Ruth Pretty's Favourite Recipes

PENGUIN BOOKS

Published by the Penguin Group

Penguin Group (NZ), 67 Apollo Drive, Rosedale,

North Shore 0632, New Zealand (a division of Pearson New Zealand Ltd)

Penguin Group (USA) Inc., 375 Hudson Street,

New York, New York 10014, USA

Penguin Group (Canada), 90 Eglinton Avenue East, Suite 700, Toronto,

Ontario, M4P 2Y3, Canada (a division of Pearson Penguin Canada Inc.)

Penguin Books Ltd, 80 Strand, London, WC2R ORL, England

Penguin Ireland, 25 St Stephen's Green,

Dublin 2, Ireland (a division of Penguin Books Ltd)

Penguin Group (Australia), 250 Camberwell Road, Camberwell,

Victoria 3124, Australia (a division of Pearson Australia Group Pty Ltd)

Penguin Books India Pvt Ltd, 11, Community Centre,

Panchsheel Park, New Delhi – 110 017, India

Penguin Books (South Africa) (Pty) Ltd, 24 Sturdee Avenue,

Rosebank, Johannesburg 2196, South Africa

Penguin Books Ltd, Registered Offices: 80 Strand, London, WC2R ORL, England

First published by Penguin Group (NZ), 2006

1 3 5 7 9 10 8 6 4 2

Designed and typeset by Seven.co.nz

Prepress by Image Centre Ltd

Printed by Everbest Printing Co. Ltd, China

ISBN – 13: 978 0 14 302090 5

ISBN – 10: 0 14 302090 0

A catalogue record for this book is available
from the National Library of New Zealand.

www.penguin.co.nz

Ruth Pretty's Favourite Recipes

Ruth Pretty

Penguin Books

Introduction

As a caterer my days are spent dreaming up ways of matching meals to situations. When a client gives me a brief, I have to come up with an idea that will wow the guests and be achievable within the circumstances. Over the last 20 years I have seen trends come and go and I have learnt that sometimes it is best to hold my tongue if a client is hell-bent on marching girls, serving staff in wetsuits, and food that is only coloured red. I try to put myself in the shoes of the guest and imagine what I would want at the party.

In all cultures, when guests are invited to your home, food and drink is offered as it is a primeval way of explaining they are welcome on your patch. The host who places food and drink at the bottom of a prioritised list is missing the whole point of a social gathering. Every host should know that the food and drink is what is remembered most commonly and for the longest time afterwards. You always hear about the food at a wedding before you hear about the bride's dress.

My mother always drummed it into me that it didn't really matter what you cooked as long as you made it tasty. Without ever saying as much she also taught me that when you cook for others it is important to do so with generosity of spirit and graciousness.

If you begin with the best possible ingredients it actually takes very little to make the food tasty. I often gaze in stunned awe at the cabinets of commercial fancy-iced cakes, elaborately piped with computer-drawn pictures or messages on the top, and wonder how anyone in their right mind would take the time to cook these monstrosities of artificial butter, cream, flavouring and colour.

This book of my favourite recipes is dedicated to my mother Betty, whom I miss very much.

Thank you, Betty

For being in the audience at the competitions
And learning the poems so you could mouth my words

For encouraging me to use the Kenwood
And showing me how to make flummery

For making me a Red Queen costume
And a White Queen costume – both with crowns

For showing me how to make salad
And letting me make it in the crystal bowl

For guiding my wrist the first time I put flour in gravy
And passing me the fish slice to take out the lumps

For unfurling the brown paper on the Christmas cake so I could pour in the brandy
And putting enough sixpences in the Christmas pudding so we all got one

For taking me to see Gracie Fields
And telling me how you danced with Alexander Grant

For breathing in while I zipped up your ballgown
And passing me a powder puff so I could put talc on your back

For whispering:
'If we all get stuck in, it won't take a minute,' and
'Whatever you do, make it tasty'

For reading me a story every night
But giving me a torch so I could read when the lights went out

Acknowledgements

I would like to thank the dedicated team at Ruth Pretty Catering for their loyalty, creativity, ability to stick to systems, attention to detail and stamina. Their hard work allows me the time to write books.

In particular, thank you to Robyn Mitchell for the work she does every day typing and formatting our recipes for publication, Jacqui Molesworth for compiling this manuscript and Renny Brown for taking so many loads off my mind. Thank you to Jo Tracey, chef in charge of the Ruth Pretty Cooking School and recipe development, for your contribution every day but in particular for your input into this book. Thank you to Pauline Graham who was our kitchen manager for so many years. Sixteen years of Pauline's common-sense freed me so I could include writing and teaching in my week.

Thank you to Bernice Beachman and Louise Armstrong my publisher and editor at Penguin respectively, to Murray Lloyd my photographer and to the team at Seven for their design work.

And lastly, thank you to my husband Paul for steering the ship.

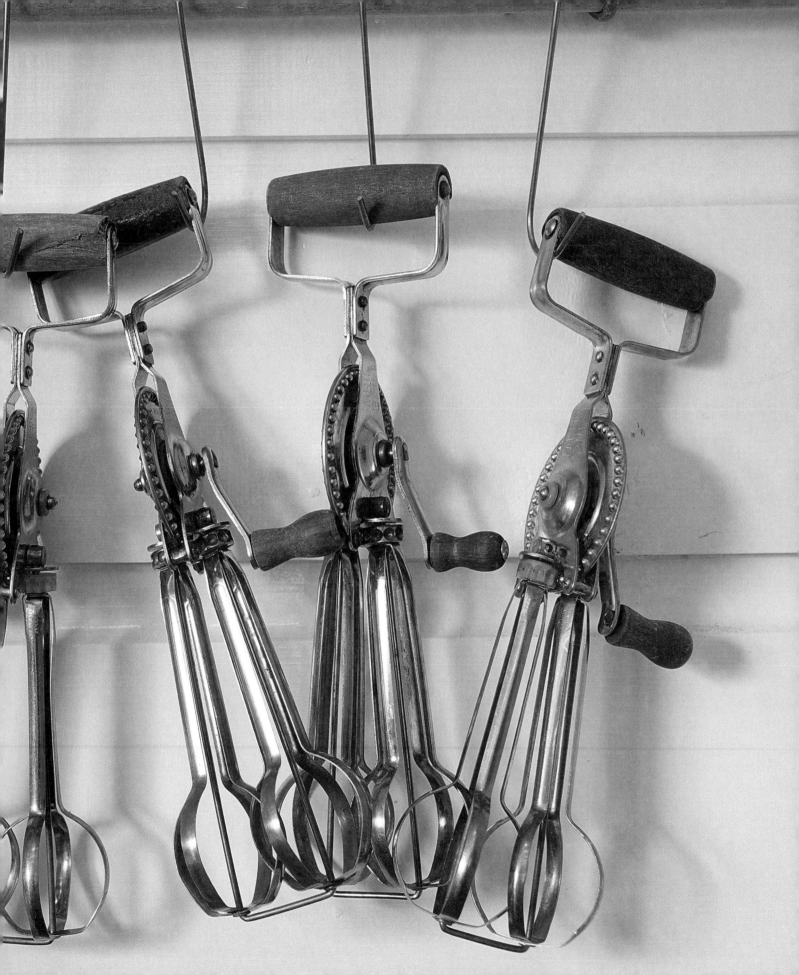

one

Starters

When friends and family are around, there is always
a certain point of the day when it is the perfect time
for a glass of wine. This chapter is dedicated to the
friends and family I like to share a glass or two of wine
with. I hope you enjoy the dishes I share with them on
those occasions.

Figlet and Walnut Cake

For 1 x 10cm round cake	For 1 x 16cm round cake
14 dried figlets (with fibrous top of stalks trimmed)	30 dried figlets (with fibrous top of stalks trimmed)
4 walnuts out of shell (lightly toasted and then quartered)	8 walnuts out of shell (lightly toasted and then quartered)
2 fresh bay leaves	4 fresh bay leaves
2 tsp fennel seeds	3 tsp fennel seeds

Figlets are very small dried figs which you will find at the supermarket. This isn't a cake in the baked sense – however, it has a cake-like shape. Accompany with a wedge of creamy blue cheese and oat biscuits.

Method

Line the base and sides of a 10 or 16cm cake tin with waxed paper.

Cut each figlet from base towards stalk, three-quarters of the way upwards, leaving stalk intact. Using your thumb, make a small indentation in the centre of each fig, being careful not to break the stalk. Place a walnut quarter into each figlet. Close figlet over and around the walnut.

Place a bay leaf, or 2 if making a larger cake, in the centre of the lined cake tin. Scatter half fennel seeds onto and around the bay leaf and push figs into mould so they fit firmly together.

Scatter figs with remaining fennel seeds and top with second bay leaf or with 2 bay leaves for the larger cake. Completely enclose the cake with waxed paper, using another sheet for the larger mould. Weight the top with a plate or bowl with a heavy jar resting on it.

Leave to sit in a cool place for 2–3 days, or up to a month, for the flavours to develop.

When ready to serve, remove cake from mould, leaving paper around cake. For decorative purposes, tie cake with a piece of cotton twine and serve whole to be opened at table.

Parmesan Chicken Skewers with Avocado and Herb Dip

Makes 20–26 cocktail-sized skewers

45g (⅓ cup) flour	35g (½ cup) finely grated Parmesan	2 tbsp olive oil
1 tsp ground flaky sea salt	1 tbsp finely chopped thyme leaves	flaky sea salt and freshly ground black pepper
freshly ground black pepper	1 tbsp finely chopped parsley leaves	2 lemons (quartered)
2 eggs	450g (10–13) chicken tenderloins	250ml Avocado and Herb Dip (see page 151)
30ml (2 tbsp) water		
100g (1½ cups) fresh breadcrumbs		

Kids will enjoy these as much as adults. Chicken tenderloin, available at the supermarket, is the elongated piece of meat which sits behind the chicken breast.

Method

Soak 20–26 wooden skewers in cold water.

In a low flat bowl, combine flour, salt and pepper. In a similar-shaped second bowl, place eggs and water and lightly whisk together. In a similar-shaped third bowl, combine breadcrumbs, Parmesan, thyme and parsley.

With a sharp knife remove thick part of sinew from each tenderloin. Cut each tenderloin in half lengthwise and thread each half onto a skewer.

Dip each chicken skewer in the flour, then egg mixture, followed by breadcrumbs. Pat breadcrumbs onto chicken to ensure even coating.

Place skewers into a container lined with plastic wrap, with plastic wrap between layers. Cover and refrigerate for a minimum of 2 hours, or overnight, so crumbs adhere well to chicken.

Heat barbecue flat plate to medium heat. Very lightly brush chicken skewers with oil. Place skewers on barbecue and cook for 3–5 minutes on each side, or until golden brown and cooked through.

Season with salt and pepper and serve with lemon wedges and Avocado and Herb Dip (see page 151).

Baked Ricotta Cake with Semi-dried Tomato and Lemon Dressing

Makes 10–15 serves

500g (2⅓ cups + 2½ tsp) ricotta

1¼ tsp flaky sea salt

baking spray or butter for greasing tray

310g Semi-dried Tomato and Lemon Dressing (see page 147)

Choose a firm ricotta for this dish. If ricotta is exuding liquid at all, place in a sieve for 30 minutes to drain. The ricotta needs to be firm to achieve a cake-shaped result.

Method

Line a 1 litre-capacity bowl with plastic wrap.

Combine ricotta with salt.

Place the ricotta in the lined bowl and press down firmly. Cover with plastic wrap and refrigerate for 3 hours.

Preheat oven to 200°C.

Grease a low-sided bun tray with baking spray or butter. Press out ricotta mould onto prepared tray. Place tray in oven and bake for 40 minutes or until golden brown. Cool and keep refrigerated until ready to use.

Remove from refrigerator at least 1 hour before serving. Lift ricotta cake onto a shallow bowl or platter and pour three-quarters of Semi-dried Tomato and Lemon Dressing over, and serve any remaining dressing on the side.

Serve with a green salad and toasted baguette or sourdough as a light meal, or as part of an antipasto platter along with cherry tomatoes, olives, crispy toast and celery sticks.

Catalan Tomato Toasts

Makes 12

3 cloves garlic

½ tsp flaky sea salt

30ml (2 tbsp) extra virgin
olive oil

½–1 sourdough loaf
(cut into 1cm-thick slices)

1kg (12) tomatoes
(very ripe and halved
widthways)

flaky sea salt and freshly
ground black pepper

additional extra virgin
olive oil

This extremely simple starter is perfect to serve at a barbecue when tomatoes are at their peak. Enter into the spirit of the occasion by encouraging DIY from your guests.

Method

Crush garlic with first measure of salt. Do this with mortar and pestle or by placing garlic and salt on a chopping board and squashing with a chef's knife laid flat to the board. Leave in mortar or place in a bowl and slowly add oil, mixing to combine.

Preheat chargrill or barbecue to hot.

Place bread slices on chargrill or barbecue, and toast both sides until golden brown.

Working quickly so toast remains warm, rub both sides of toast with tomatoes, squeezing tomato halves slightly as you rub, leaving seeds and juice on the toast.

Drizzle or spread both sides of toast with garlic oil mixture and sprinkle top side with salt and pepper. Serve immediately, offering additional extra virgin olive oil on the side.

Herbed Cream Cheese and Vegetable Sandwiches

Makes 20 cocktail-sized sandwiches

250g (1 cup) cream cheese (at room temperature)

¼ cup finely chopped Italian parsley

1 tbsp finely chopped marjoram

2 tsp finely chopped chervil

flaky sea salt and freshly ground black pepper

50g (½) carrot (peeled)

60g (2–3) radishes

100g (⅓) cucumber (skin on if tender)

1 ficelle (mini baguette) (cut into 7mm thick slices)

A ficelle is an excellent size, sliced, for easy-to-eat cocktail-sized sandwiches. These are best eaten fresh but if preparing ahead of time, for example in the morning, store in an airtight container in the refrigerator, with greaseproof paper between each layer, and bring out of the refrigerator at least 30 minutes before serving.

Method

In a medium-sized bowl, place cream cheese, parsley, marjoram and chervil. Add salt and pepper to taste. Mash with a fork to combine.

Coarsely grate carrot, radishes and cucumber separately.

Place carrot onto one half of a clean, dry tea towel (or paper towel), cover with the remaining half and press firmly to release moisture into tea towel.

Repeat this process with the radish.

Follow the same steps for the cucumber, but instead of pressing on the tea towel, wring it out as cucumber contains a lot more moisture.

Lay out ficelle slices on a chopping board and spread each slice with a teaspoonful of the Herbed Cream Cheese. Top each ficelle slice with a little mound of one of the vegetables, or a mixture of the vegetables.

Season to taste with salt and pepper. Gently top with second slice of ficelle. Do not press down on sandwiches.

Serve on the day they are made.

Chicken Liver Pâté

Makes 500g / Serves 8–10

450g chicken livers (trimmed of green-tinged parts and sinew)

45g (3 tbsp) unsalted butter

2 shallots (peeled and chopped)

100g (4 small) rashers rindless bacon (diced)

1 tsp roughly chopped thyme leaves

1 tsp roughly chopped rosemary leaves

1 clove garlic (peeled and crushed to a cream with salt)

flaky sea salt and freshly ground black pepper

1½ tsp honey

1 tbsp Armagnac or Cognac

extra virgin olive oil or melted clarified butter

Chicken Liver Pâté is a perennial. Serve with toasted Vogel's bread, little gherkins and radishes. If the quantity is too large for one sitting then divide into several smaller dishes to have on hand to use over several days.

Method

Rinse livers gently in cold water and drain.

In a heavy-based frying pan melt butter over a medium heat. Add shallots and bacon. Cook until shallots are soft and transparent and bacon is rendering its fat.

Add thyme, rosemary, garlic and livers. Cook gently, stirring occasionally until livers have turned pale brown, are still pink inside and have become a little firm.

Season to taste with salt and pepper and stir in honey and Armagnac or Cognac.

Pour contents of frying pan into bowl of a food processor with metal blade fitted and purée until smooth. Place purée in a sieve and, using the back of a soup ladle, press purée through sieve. Discard any fibre left in sieve.

Taste for seasoning and pour into a shallow dish to cool. To prevent surface from oxidising, brush with oil or clarified butter, then cover with plastic wrap and refrigerate until required.

1.

2.

3.

Herbed Yoghurt Dip with Pita Crisps and Toasted Walnuts

Serves 8–10

130g (½ cup) Greek-style yoghurt

45g (3 tbsp + 2 tsp) ricotta

45g (4½ tbsp) cream cheese (softened in microwave on medium heat for 20 seconds)

¼ cup chopped French tarragon leaves

3 tbsp finely chopped chives

45ml (3 tbsp) olive oil

30ml (2 tbsp) lemon juice

finely grated zest of 1 lemon

flaky sea salt and freshly ground white pepper

Pita Crisps

50g (24) toasted walnut halves

Pita Crisps

1 packet pita bread

45ml (3 tbsp) olive oil

flaky sea salt

This is a very fresh-tasting dip. You may wish to substitute the herbs listed above for other herbs you have in your garden. However, plant French tarragon in a frost-free spot for harvesting in summer to really enjoy this dip.

Method

Mix together yoghurt, ricotta and cream cheese. Add tarragon, chives, oil, lemon juice and lemon zest with salt and pepper to taste and stir well. Cover with plastic wrap and leave to sit in the refrigerator for 2–4 hours for flavours to infuse.

Serve with Pita Crisps and toasted walnuts.

The triangular shape of these crisps makes a very convenient dipper. Make fresh as required as the oil will taste rancid after several days.

To Make Pita Crisps

Preheat oven to 180°C.

Cut pita breads horizontally through centre. Brush both cut sides with oil and sprinkle with salt.

Cut pita bread halves into 6 or 8 wedges. Place on a baking tray and bake for 5–8 minutes, or until light golden brown.

Eat immediately, or store in an airtight container for up to 2 days.

1. Herbed Yoghurt Dip with Pita Crisps and Toasted Walnuts
3. Herbed Cream Cheese and Vegetable Sandwiches (see page 18)
2. Kumara Dip with Celery Sticks (see page 22)
4. Chicken Liver Pâté (see page 19)

Kumara Dip with Celery Sticks

Makes 10–15 serves

300g (2) golden kumara (peeled and roughly chopped)

½ tsp flaky sea salt

2 thick slices stale white bread (crusts removed)

100ml (⅓ cup + 1 tbsp) milk

1 clove garlic (chopped)

30ml (2 tbsp) lemon juice

¼ tsp flaky sea salt

white pepper to taste

100ml (⅓ cup + 1 tbsp) extra virgin olive oil

additional extra virgin olive oil

30–45 cocktail-sized celery sticks

I like to mound this dip into a bowl and make an indent to hold a well of extra virgin olive oil. This dip also makes a very tasty accompaniment to hot or cold lamb.

Method

Place kumara in a saucepan, with water to cover and add salt. Place over a medium heat and simmer until tender. Drain and cool.

Place bread in a bowl and add milk. Leave to sit for 5 minutes or until milk has been absorbed.

In a food processor fitted with a metal blade, place kumara, bread, garlic, lemon juice, salt and pepper and process until smooth.

With the motor running, very slowly pour oil through the feed tube as you would for mayonnaise. This dip should be creamy and smooth.

Spoon into a serving bowl and drizzle with additional oil. Accompany with celery sticks.

Barbecued Prawns with Chermoula Paste

Serves 10–15 for pre-dinner drinks

¼ cup firmly packed, roughly chopped Italian parsley leaves

3 tbsp firmly packed, roughly chopped coriander leaves

3 cloves garlic (peeled and chopped)

¾ tsp sweet smoked Spanish paprika

2 tsp ground cumin

2 tsp ground coriander

¼ tsp cayenne pepper

1 tbsp lemon juice

2 tbsp olive oil

30 large prawns (peeled and heads removed but tails intact)

olive oil for barbecue

flaky sea salt

juice of 1–2 limes

These spicy prawns will be popular so you may wish to increase the quantity, particularly if served with bubbly or a crisp sauvignon blanc. Prawns can be substituted with scampi tails.

Method

Place parsley, coriander leaves, garlic, paprika, cumin, ground coriander, cayenne pepper, lemon juice and oil in a food processor fitted with a metal blade and process until a paste is formed. Transfer to a large bowl.

Rub Chermoula Paste into prawns.

Heat a barbecue, flat plate or heavy-based frying pan to hot. Smear flat plate with a little oil and place prawns on it, being careful not to overcrowd the plate. Cook for 1–2 minutes on each side until prawns are golden brown and cooked through.

Remove and serve sprinkled with salt and lime juice.

Scallops à la Provençale

Makes 12 teaser serves or 6 entrée serves

60g (6 tbsp) unsalted butter (diced)

70g (½ cup) peeled and finely chopped shallots

560g (36) scallops

1 clove garlic (finely chopped)

flaky sea salt and freshly ground black pepper

100ml (⅓ cup + 1 tbsp) sauvignon blanc

2 tbsp finely chopped tarragon leaves

2 tbsp finely chopped parsley leaves

2 handfuls baby salad greens (optional)

1–2 lemons (halved)

Sometimes the simplest dishes are the best. Make the most of fresh scallops when they are in season. Treat scallops very gently when you cook them, using a spatula rather than tongs so that the scallops are not pierced or torn.

Method

In a heavy-based frying pan over a medium heat, melt butter until bubbling.

Add shallots and cook for 2–3 minutes or until they begin to soften.

Add scallops and garlic, then salt and pepper to taste. Cook for a further 2–3 minutes or until scallops are just about cooked and shallots are soft.

Add wine and cook for a further 2 minutes, or until scallops are cooked and liquid has reduced by one-third.

Remove frying pan from heat, add herbs to mixture and toss through.

If you wish, line platter or small plates with baby salad greens, place scallops on platter or plates then drizzle with pan juices. Season to taste with lemon juice and salt and pepper. Serve.

two

Family Dinners

You don't need a reason to invite friends and family over for dinner. It can just be for the fun of it: a chance to spend time together, perhaps watch a rugby game or to cap off a big day out. However, the cook always needs to be prepared. Family Dinners is a collection of my favourite recipes which are all about preparing ahead so there is very little to do at dinner time.

The Stewart Family Chowder

Serves 8–10

30g (3 tbsp) unsalted butter	650g (2) potatoes (peeled and diced)	250ml (1 cup) cream
80g (2–3) rindless bacon rashers (diced)	170g (2–3) stalks celery (finely diced)	700g firm flesh white fish such as groper (hapuka) or blue cod (cubed)
500g (2) large onions (diced)	1 tsp freshly ground white pepper	¾ cup finely chopped Italian parsley
1 bay leaf	1.25l (5 cups) water	1½ tsp flaky sea salt
21g (3 tbsp) flour	250ml (1 cup) milk	

This milky white fish chowder was a recipe given to me by my friend Bronwen Stewart. It is a recipe a young teacher at her rural primary school in Hawke's Bay had brought back from New England, USA and given to Bronwen's mother. It was a favourite in the Stewart household. For a chowder it actually has a simple list of ingredients but it is surprisingly big on flavour.

Method

In a heavy-based saucepan melt butter over a medium heat.

Add bacon, onion and bay leaf and cook, stirring from time to time until onion is soft and transparent.

Add flour and combine well, stirring for 2–3 minutes over a medium heat until flour smells nutty.

Add potatoes and celery and toss around in saucepan until they are coated with the onion mixture. Stir ingredients to prevent them sticking to base of saucepan.

Add pepper and water, cover with a lid and bring to a simmer. Continue to simmer until potatoes are cooked but still retain their shape. At this stage, you can set aside until you are almost ready to serve.

Pour milk and cream into saucepan and stir until just below boiling point. Add fish and parsley.

Stirring frequently, heat to just before boiling point, making sure chowder does not boil.

Check potatoes and fish are cooked, add salt to taste and serve immediately.

Francie's Lasagne with Italian Sausage and Ricotta

Serves 8–10

250g (4) Italian-style pork sausages flavoured with fennel seed

30ml (2 tbsp) olive oil (+ extra for greasing dish)

750g lean coarse beef mince

180g (1 medium) onion (finely chopped)

2 cloves garlic (finely chopped)

20g (2 tbsp) sugar

2 tbsp roughly chopped basil leaves

2 tbsp finely chopped oregano leaves

2 tbsp finely chopped Italian parsley leaves

flaky sea salt and freshly ground black pepper

1.2kg (3 x 400g tins) whole peeled Italian tomatoes in their juice (roughly chopped)

300g (1 tin) tomato paste

312g (1½ cups) ricotta

1 egg (lightly beaten)

2 tbsp finely chopped Italian parsley

1.5kg–2kg (6–8) fresh or dried lasagne sheets

250g fresh mozzarella (drained and thinly sliced)

100g (1½ cups) finely grated Parmesan

This is the dish my friend Francie Shagin likes to prepare when she and her husband Terry invite friends over to watch rugby. It is made entirely in advance, and if time is pressured Francie will make and freeze it ahead. Seek out Italian-style pork sausages flavoured with fennel seed from a speciality store or market.

Method

Remove sausage meat from skins. Discard skins.

Heat a large frying pan over a high heat, add 1 tbsp oil and cook sausage meat for 3–4 minutes on each side or until browned and almost cooked through. Remove from frying pan and drain on paper towels. Cut into 1cm cubes.

Over a medium heat, in a medium to large saucepan, place 1 tbsp oil and when hot add beef mince, onion and garlic. Cook, breaking up mince with a wooden spoon, until mince is browned and onion is soft.

Add sausages, sugar, basil, oregano, first measure of parsley, salt and pepper to taste, tomatoes and their juice, and tomato paste. Bring to the boil, reduce heat to a simmer and cook for 15–20 minutes, or until thick and a wooden spoon stands up in the centre of the saucepan. Remove mixture to a bowl and cool.

In a small bowl, place ricotta, egg, second measure of parsley with salt and pepper to taste and combine.

Lightly grease a 29 x 22cm lasagne dish (or similar) with olive oil and spoon in a quarter of meat mixture. Top with a layer of lasagne sheets. You may need to cut lasagne sheets to fit. Spread with one-third of ricotta mixture. Top with one-third of the mozzarella cheese and a sprinkle of Parmesan.

Cover Parmesan with second quarter of meat mixture. Continue to layer with lasagne sheets, ricotta mixture and cheeses until you have 3 layers of each (retaining a little for the top).

Complete lasagne with a final layer of meat and sprinkle with remaining Parmesan. Store in refrigerator or freezer or proceed to next step.

Preheat oven to 200°C.

Cover lasagne loosely with aluminium foil and place in oven for 30 minutes, or 40 minutes if the lasagne has come out of refrigerator. Frozen lasagne will need to be thawed before it goes into the oven.

Reduce oven temperature to 180°C.

Remove aluminium foil and cook lasagne for a further 20–25 minutes until lasagne is hot in the centre and cheese on top is golden brown.

Portion into large squares and serve accompanied by salad if you wish.

Photograph on following page: Francie's Lasagne with Italian Sausage and Ricotta

Springfield Roast Chicken with Tomato and Toasted Sourdough Salad

Serves 4–6

1.8kg (size 18) chicken (corn-fed or organic, preferably)

4 sprigs sage

½ tbsp ground flaky sea salt

½ tsp freshly ground black pepper

Tomato and Toasted Sourdough Salad (see page 80)

Jus

250ml (1 cup) chardonnay

15ml (1 tbsp) balsamic vinegar

flaky sea salt and freshly ground black pepper

30g (3 tbsp) diced unsalted cold butter (optional)

Kosher chickens are extremely moist, succulent birds. However, in New Zealand kosher chickens are just regular commercial chickens which in the killing process are salted, often referred to as brined, to make them 'clean'. This recipe, which includes salting the chicken before roasting, is adapted from *The Zuni Café Cookbook* by Judy Rodgers and will produce an extremely tasty, moist and succulent roast chicken with crispy skin. You do need to salt the chicken at least one day or up to three days ahead.

Method

Rinse chicken under cold running water, then dry thoroughly inside and out.

Slide a finger under skin of each breast to make 2 pockets. Turn chicken over to make 2 more pockets on the outside of thickest section of each thigh.

Using your fingers push a sprig of sage into each pocket.

Liberally sprinkle chicken with salt and pepper, retaining a little salt for inside cavity.

Twist and tuck wing tips behind the shoulders. Cross and tie legs together with cotton twine.

Cover chicken loosely with plastic wrap and refrigerate overnight, or for up to 3 days.

Preheat oven to 230°C. Using paper towels pat chicken dry. Do not rinse.

Place a heavy-based, ovenproof frying pan or heavy roasting tray in oven until it is hot. (I always use my cast-iron Aga frying pan.)

Place chicken, breast-side up, into hot pan. It should sizzle. Place in oven and cook for 45–50 minutes. If skin begins to burn during this time, turn chicken over with a fish slice, return to oven and continue to cook.

Photograph on previous page: Springfield Roast Chicken

Cook for a further 10–15 minutes, or until skin is crisp and meat juices run clear. Total cooking time will be 50 minutes to 1 hour.

Remove chicken from oven and, using a fish slice, lift chicken from pan onto a warm platter. Cover with aluminium foil and leave chicken to rest for 10–15 minutes.

To Make Jus

Drain clear fat from frying pan, leaving any lean dripping in pan. Place pan over a medium heat and add wine. Stir well. Reduce liquid by half, add vinegar and bring back to the boil, then reduce heat and season to taste.

If you wish to soften the flavour of the jus, add butter piece by piece over a low heat, whisking as you add.

To Serve

Chop chicken into portions. Place a large spoonful of Tomato and Toasted Sourdough Salad (see page 80) in the centre of each plate and nestle chicken on top. Accompany with jus served in a jug.

Method for Cooking in Wood-fired Oven

Prepare oven as for cooking flat bread or pizza. (In other words, you need an extremely hot wood-fired oven.) Cooking method is the same as oven method. Cooking time will be similar but move pan around now and again to prevent the side of the chicken which is facing the embers from burning. The wood-fired oven chicken will have a slightly darker skin and an even better flavour.

Osso Bucco

Serves 4

50g (5 tbsp) butter

115g (1) small onion (finely chopped)

320–360g (3) medium carrots (peeled and finely diced)

120–130g (2) small celery sticks (finely chopped)

1 clove garlic (finely chopped)

3 strips lemon peel (white pith removed)

70–140g (½–1 cup) flour

1.5–1.65kg (8) 4cm-thick veal shanks (prepared by butcher in the Osso Bucco style)

75ml (5 tbsp) olive oil

250ml (1 cup) chardonnay

250ml (1 cup) beef stock

400g (1 tin) whole, peeled Italian tomatoes in their juice (roughly chopped)

½ tsp finely chopped thyme leaves

2 bay leaves

3–4 parsley sprigs

flaky sea salt and freshly ground black pepper

Osso Bucco has to be one of the tastiest winter meals you can make. Prepare and cook one, two or even three days before serving. Order the veal shanks ahead from your butcher. Choose a very large casserole dish, as the veal shanks need to sit in a single layer. I use a 30cm-diameter Le Creuset casserole dish.

Method

Preheat oven to 180°C.

In a large, heavy-based casserole dish, melt butter over a medium heat. Add onion, carrots and celery and cook, stirring occasionally, for 6–7 minutes or until onion is soft but not coloured.

Add garlic and lemon peel and cook for a further 2–3 minutes or until vegetables are softened. Remove from heat.

Tip flour onto a plate and toss veal shanks in flour to coat, shaking off any excess.

Heat a heavy-based frying pan over a medium-high heat and add some of the oil.

When oil is hot, add veal shanks but do not overcrowd the pan. Brown thoroughly. Repeat process with remaining oil and shanks. Remove shanks from pan using a slotted spoon and place on top of vegetables in casserole dish.

Tip away excess oil from frying pan. Pour wine into pan and simmer over a medium heat until reduced by half, at the same time scraping the base and sides of pan to remove any cooking residues. Pour over shanks in casserole dish.

Add stock, tomatoes, thyme, bay leaves, parsley with salt and pepper to taste, bring to a simmer, then add to casserole …

... Osso Bucco

Chargrilled Lamb Chops, Spanish-style

Serves 4–6

65ml (¼ cup) olive oil

3 cloves garlic (crushed)

2 tbsp Italian parsley (finely chopped)

flaky sea salt and freshly ground black pepper

12–24 small lamb chops (cut from a premium Frenched lamb rack. Do not trim any further, i.e. leave silver skin on. Number depends on size of chops and appetites of guests. There are 8 chops per rack)

Iceberg Salad from La Rioja (see page 76)

…The liquid should cover two-thirds of the depth of shanks. If it doesn't, add a little more stock.

Over a medium heat, bring casserole to a simmer. Add lid to casserole and place in lower half of the preheated oven.

Cook for 2 hours, or until meat feels very tender when prodded with a fork, and sauce has thickened. Turn shanks approximately every 20 minutes during cooking so they brown evenly. If there is insufficient liquid for serving, thin it down with a little water. Taste for seasoning.

To Serve

Present veal shanks with sauce and vegetables poured over the shanks. Accompany with mashed potatoes, noodles or rice and green vegetables or salad.

Seek out the smallest lamb chops you can find. Provided you have organised ingredients in advance, there is very little work involved in the preparation and cooking of this dish.

Method

Heat chargrill or barbecue to a high temperature.

In a small bowl, combine olive oil, garlic and parsley.

Grind salt and pepper onto chops. Dip chops in marinade and rub marinade into meat for a few seconds.

Place onto hot grill and, for small Frenched lamb chops, cook for 3 minutes on each side or until medium-rare.

Remove from grill, place onto a warmed tray and cover with a heavy tea towel to rest for 5 minutes. Serve with salad.

Savoury Bread and Butter Pudding

Serves 5–6

30g (3 tbsp) unsalted butter (melted) (+ extra for greasing dish)

6 eggs

125ml (½ cup) milk

125ml (½ cup) cream

1 tsp Sicilian red chilli flakes

½ sourdough loaf or ½ loaf sliced white bread (crusts removed – once crusts have been removed, weight should be about 200g)

50g (¾ cup) finely grated Parmesan

120g (1 cup) grated cheddar (aged cheddar if possible)

flaky sea salt and freshly ground white pepper

1 tbsp chopped chives

This handy dish is quick to prepare and, once prepared, you leave it to sit for up to six hours, or overnight, and then bake when ready to serve. It can be enjoyed at brunch or lunch, or when you need supper rather than dinner. The best result is when you use sourdough bread. Serve with a salad or enjoy with asparagus when in season.

Method

Grease a 1.25-litre baking dish, or similar, with baking spray or melted butter.

In a large bowl, place eggs, milk, cream and chilli flakes and whisk together to combine.

Cut bread into 2.5cm cubes and set aside.

Combine cheeses in a bowl and sprinkle a third of cheese mixture onto base of baking dish. Form a layer of bread on top, using about half the bread, cover with second layer of cheese and season. Repeat with a second layer of bread and top with remaining cheese. Season well.

Pour egg mixture evenly over bread and cheese. Drizzle with butter.

Cover with plastic wrap and refrigerate overnight, or for at least 6 hours.

Preheat oven to 180°C and bake for about 20–25 minutes until egg mixture is cooked and pudding is puffed and golden in colour.

Sprinkle with chives and serve immediately.

1.

2.

3.

Bean and Chorizo Soup

Serves 8–10

2 bay leaves

8 parsley stalks

30ml (2 tbsp) olive oil

180g (1) medium onion (finely diced)

10 cloves garlic (peeled and halved)

220g (1) pig's trotter

250g (1) lamb shank

1.75l (7 cups) water

430g dried, non-heat-treated haricot beans (soaked overnight and drained)

250g (1) large starchy potato, preferably Agria (peeled and broken into 3–4cm pieces)

120g chorizo sausage (cut into 5mm slices)

1½ tsp sweet smoked Spanish paprika

2 tbsp finely chopped, bottled piquillo peppers, or grilled and peeled red peppers

2cm piece dried red chilli (roughly chopped)

115g (3) tomatoes (peeled, deseeded and chopped)

2 tbsp finely chopped Italian parsley

flaky sea salt and freshly ground black pepper

15ml (1 tbsp) sherry vinegar

This is more of a stew than a soup so can be enjoyed as starter or as a main course. It is a very creamy soup partly because of the haricot beans but also because of the breaking of the starchy potato. To break a potato plunge the tail end of a soup spoon into the potato to crack it and then break potato into pieces with your hands. It is important to cook this soup very slowly. It is also much better eaten at least a day after it is made.

Method

Tie bay leaves and parsley stalks together with cotton twine.

In a large, heavy-based saucepan or cast-iron casserole dish, heat oil over a medium heat. Add onion, garlic, pig's trotter, lamb shank, bay leaves and parsley stalks. Sauté until onion and garlic are soft and lamb shank is browned on all sides (about 5–6 minutes).

Add water and beans. Cover with a lid and bring to the boil. Reduce heat and simmer for 30 minutes. (A SimmerMat placed under the saucepan will prevent mixture from catching.)

Add potato, chorizo, paprika, peppers, chilli, tomatoes, parsley, salt and pepper, and simmer with the lid on for a further 50–60 minutes, or until potatoes and beans are creamy soft. (Once again a SimmerMat will be useful.)

Turn off heat, stir in sherry vinegar and let rest for 30 minutes, or overnight for optimum flavour.

Remove pig's trotter and discard. Remove lamb shank and remove all meat from bone. Cut meat into bite-size pieces and return to soup. Discard bone. Remove bay leaves and parsley stalks and discard.

Reheat gradually, stirring often, until soup is hot. Taste for seasoning and serve.

1. Savoury Bread and Butter Pudding (see page 39)   2. Chargrilled Lamb Chops, Spanish-style (see page 38) with Iceberg Salad from La Rioja (see page 76)

3. Bean and Chorizo Soup

Roasted Eggplant, Red Pepper and Zucchini Lasagne with Puy Lentils

Serves 6–8

olive oil for greasing dish

625ml (2½ cups) Garlic Béchamel Sauce (see page 152)

45g (¼ cup) Puy lentils (cooked to instructions on packet)

1kg (4–5) fresh or dried lasagne sheets

250g (1) eggplant (cut into 7.5mm thick rounds, tossed in olive oil, hot-roasted at 220°C until soft through and golden brown on the edges)

150ml (1½ cup + 1 tbsp + 1 tsp) Fresh Tomato Sauce (see page 146), (or use a fresh commercial variety, which may be called pasta sauce)

520g (4) red peppers (roasted, skinned and cut into 1.5cm strips)

30ml (2 tbsp) Basil Pesto (see page 153 or use a fresh commercial variety)

500g (5–6) zucchini (cut lengthwise into very thin strips, tossed in olive oil, hot-roasted at 220°C until soft and golden brown on the edges)

90g (¾ cup) grated tasty cheese

35g (½ cup) finely grated Parmesan

This dish, full of flavour and texture, is adored by vegetarians and meat-eaters alike. It is prepared ahead and cooked prior to being served. The preparation does require two sauces and pesto, which can be made in advance and, if required, frozen. When making sauces and pesto prepare extra to freeze for next time.

Method

Lightly grease the base and sides of a 29 x 22cm lasagne dish, or similar, with oil.

Spread 125ml (½ cup) Garlic Béchamel Sauce over the base of the dish.

Divide lentils into 3 portions and sprinkle sauce with a portion of lentils. Cover with a single layer of lasagne sheets. You may need to cut lasagne sheets to fit.

Lay eggplant on top of lasagne sheets and cover with 125ml (½ cup) Garlic Béchamel Sauce.

Top with second portion of lentils and cover with a single layer of lasagne sheets.

Cover lasagne sheets with Fresh Tomato Sauce and top with peppers.

Cover peppers with a single layer of lasagne sheets and spread evenly with Basil Pesto.

Lay zucchini onto pesto and top with 85ml (⅓ cup) Garlic Béchamel Sauce and remainder of lentils.

Top with a final single layer of lasagne sheets and remainder of Garlic Béchamel Sauce. Sprinkle with cheeses. Store in refrigerator for up to 2 days, or proceed to the next step.

Preheat oven to 190°C.

Place in oven and bake for 30–40 minutes until lasagne is soft and top is golden brown.

Cut lasagne into generous portions and accompany with salad if you wish.

Chicken and Pistachio Pies

Makes 3 x 10cm raised pies

Chicken and Pistachio
Pie Filling

baking spray or melted
butter for greasing tins

flour for rolling pastry

Cream Cheese Pastry
(see page 47)

egg wash (1 lightly beaten
egg yolk mixed with 1 tbsp
water)

9 fresh sage leaves (washed
and stems removed)

500ml (2 cups) chicken
stock

reserved soaking liquid
from cranberries in
Chicken and Pistachio
Pie Filling

Chicken and Pistachio Pie Filling

50ml (3 tbsp + 1 tsp)
chicken stock

15g (2 tbsp) dried
cranberries

30ml (2 tbsp) olive oil

325g chicken tenderloin
(tendon removed, diced)

90g (½) onion (finely
diced)

1 clove garlic (finely
chopped)

175g ham in 1 piece
off the bone (diced)

40g (¼ cup) pistachio nuts
(toasted and roughly
chopped)

4 tsp finely chopped
sage leaves

1 tsp finely grated
orange zest

¾ tsp flaky sea salt

½ tsp freshly ground
black pepper

Making three small pies rather than one large pie makes sense as rather than having part of a pie left over, you will have 'a pie' left over for another meal. If you prefer one large pie, use a 17cm springform cake tin. Begin to cook the large pie at 200°C, then after 20 minutes reduce temperature to 180°C and cook for a further 25–35 minutes. At Christmas-time make these pies with turkey.

Method

Make the Chicken and Pistachio Pie Filling.

Grease 3 x 10cm springform cake tins with baking spray or melted butter.

Lightly flour pastry bench and roll pastry to 2mm thickness.

Using an 18cm cake tin-base as a guide, cut out 3 pastry bases.

Using the 10cm pie tin base as a guide, cut out 3 pastry lids, adding on 1cm all around to allow for rolling the edge.

Cut a 5mm–1cm hole to act as an air vent in the centre of each pastry lid.

Push bases into prepared tins leaving a 1cm overhang at the top.

Fill bases with Chicken and Pistachio Pie Filling to about three-quarters full.

Using a pastry brush, brush under-side edges of pastry lids with water and place on top of filled bases.

Press edges together using your fingers and roll pastry over on an angle towards the centre of pie to seal edges and form a neatly rolled edge.

Rest pies in refrigerator for 20–30 minutes.

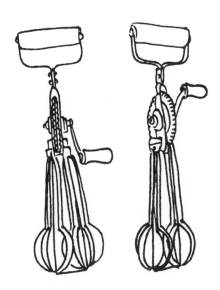

Preheat oven to 190°C.

Brush tops and rolled edge with egg wash. Arrange 3 sage leaves on each pie and brush egg wash over top, to help leaves adhere to pastry.

Bake in oven for 30–40 minutes until pastry is golden brown and cooked. Cool.

Pour chicken stock and reserved soaking liquid from cranberries in Chicken and Pistachio Pie Filling into a medium-sized saucepan, place over a medium heat and bring to the boil. Reduce heat and simmer until stock has reduced by two-thirds. Cool.

Pour stock into a squeeze bottle and squeeze enough stock into each pie, through the hole in the lid, to come up to the top of pie. Refrigerate pies until stock has jellied.

To Make Chicken and Pistachio Pie Filling

Heat stock in a saucepan over a medium heat and warm to just below boiling point. Remove from heat.

Add cranberries and soak until stock becomes cold, or until you are ready to proceed.

Heat a heavy-based frying pan over a medium heat, pour in oil and heat until hot. Add chicken and gently toss around in oil. Cook for 3–4 minutes, or until chicken is half cooked. Add onion and garlic and cook for 3–4 minutes, or until onion is soft but not brown and chicken is fully cooked.

Transfer to a large bowl and cool.

Drain cranberries and reserve liquid.

Add ham, pistachios, cranberries, sage, orange zest, salt and pepper to chicken mixture and combine.

Cream Cheese Pastry

Makes 630g

285g (2 cups + 1 tbsp) flour
(+ extra for dusting board)

¼ tsp baking powder

125g (½ cup) cream cheese

170g unsalted butter
(diced)

30ml (2 tbsp) iced water

15ml (1 tbsp) cider vinegar

Tina Duncan, from White Tie Catering in Christchurch, gave me her favourite pastry recipe based on Rose Beranbaum's recipe from *The Pie and Pastry Bible*. It is deliciously rich, very easy to work and holds its shape well. Make extra to freeze.

Method

Place flour and baking powder in the bowl of a food processor fitted with a metal blade and pulse.

Chop cream cheese into 5–6 pieces and add to flour. Process until coarsely chopped.

Add butter and process until butter is the size of small peas.

Add water and vinegar and process until dough just begins to come together.

Tip onto a lightly floured board. Gently knead together by hand. Work into a ball and flatten with the palm of your hand.

Wrap in plastic wrap and rest in refrigerator for 1 hour, or overnight.

Chicken and Pistachio Pies (see page 44)

Roasted Mushroom and Lemon Thyme Galette

Serves 6–8

500g (8) Portobello mushrooms (cut into 1cm slices)

500g (24–28) white button mushrooms (halved or, if large, quartered)

500g (28–32) Swiss brown mushrooms (thickly sliced)

125ml (½ cup) olive oil

4 tbsp (¼ cup) finely chopped lemon thyme leaves

flaky sea salt and freshly ground black pepper

flour for dusting bench

550g puff pastry (the most buttery version you can buy)

125g (½ cup) cream cheese (diced)

20g (4 tbsp) finely grated Parmesan

1 egg (lightly beaten)

15ml (1 tbsp) lemon juice

zest of 1 lemon

3 spring onions (white parts roughly chopped)

1 egg (separated)

15ml (1 tbsp) water

shaved Parmesan to garnish (optional)

This is a satisfying prepare-ahead dish which works a trick accompanied with a buttery chardonnay and a rocket salad.

Method

Preheat oven to 210°C.

Toss mushrooms in olive oil and thyme. Sprinkle generously with salt and pepper and place on a low-sided baking tray.

Place in oven and roast for 8–10 minutes until mushrooms are soft and juicy. Drain the cooking juices (discard or save for another use) and cool mushrooms.

Taste for seasoning.

Very lightly sprinkle flour onto pastry bench and roll out pastry to a 45–47cm round. Place round onto a low-sided baking tray and place in refrigerator for at least 30 minutes.

Place cream cheese, Parmesan, egg, lemon juice, lemon zest and spring onions into a bowl and combine, using a wooden spoon. Add salt and pepper to taste.

Spread cream cheese mixture onto the centre of the pastry round leaving an 8cm border. Pile roasted mushrooms on top of the cream cheese mixture.

Place egg white in a bowl and beat lightly with a fork. Brush egg white around pastry border and fold pastry, pleating as you go, to partially cover the mushrooms.

Rest galette for 30 minutes in refrigerator, or overnight.

Place egg yolk in a small bowl with water and combine with a fork to make an egg wash. Brush pastry with egg wash, place in oven and bake for 25–30 minutes, or until pastry is cooked through and golden brown. If pastry begins to look too brown on the top of the galette during the cooking time, loosely cover galette with aluminium foil.

Rest for at least 15 minutes before slicing. Serve hot, warm or cold. If you wish, sprinkle with shaved Parmesan.

Jo Tracey's Meat Loaf

Serves 6

600g minced beef (topside, rump or chuck)

400g pure pork sausage meat

175g (1½ cups) peeled and grated carrots

150g (1 cup) peeled and grated apples

2 eggs (lightly beaten)

30ml (2 tbsp) olive oil

200g (2 small) onions (finely diced)

2 cloves garlic (finely chopped)

125ml (½ cup) Old-fashioned Tomato Sauce (see page 147), your favourite chutney or tomato pasta sauce

15ml (1 tbsp) Worcestershire sauce

30ml (2 tbsp) Thai sweet chilli sauce

2 tbsp finely chopped parsley

2 tsp finely chopped thyme leaves

flaky sea salt and freshly ground black pepper

120g (4) rindless bacon rashers

Accompany this extremely tasty meat loaf – an absolute favourite in Jo Tracey's household – with what else but mashed potatoes and broccoli or beans. Hopefully you will have lots left over for sandwiches.

Method

In a large bowl, combine minced beef, sausage meat, carrots, apples and eggs.

Heat oil in a small frying pan over a medium heat. Add onions and cook until onions are soft and transparent but not browned. Add garlic and cook a further 1 minute, or until onions are soft but not browned. Remove from heat and cool.

Add onion mixture to meat mixture. Add half tomato sauce, Worcestershire sauce, chilli sauce, parsley and thyme. Add salt and pepper to taste and mix well. Cook a tiny ball of mixture in microwave to taste for seasoning.

Push mixture into 26 x 8cm loaf tin and smooth top down with cold wet hands. Pour remaining ¼ cup tomato sauce over mixture and spread to cover. Cut bacon into lengths the same width as loaf tin and lay widthways, slightly overlapping, along the top of the tomato sauce. At this stage you can refrigerate for up to one day.

Preheat oven to 180°C.

Place in oven. Bake for 1 hour 20 minutes, or until cooked through. Remove from oven and rest, covered with a clean tea towel, for 10–15 minutes. If you wish, pour off any fat juices from loaf pan.

When ready to serve, tip meat loaf out of loaf tin and slice. A serrated-edged knife will make cutting through bacon easier. Serve hot, warm or cold.

three

Celebration Dinners

This is the chapter for the big occasion – when you assemble
friends and family together to make an announcement, or to
celebrate a birthday or Christmas. All the following recipes
are absolute favourites of mine, and guaranteed to fill the
house with mouth-watering aromas.

Soy, Star Anise and Ginger Whole-baked Salmon

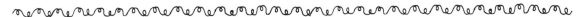

Serves 15–20

2.5–3kg (1) whole fresh salmon (washed and dried)

Soy, Star Anise and Ginger Marinade

lime halves to garnish

Soy, Star Anise and Ginger Marinade – Makes 475ml

50g (6) 2–3 cm pieces ginger (peeled and finely julienned)

20 whole star anise

310ml (1¼ cups) light soy sauce such as Tamari

7g (1 tbsp) grated palm sugar

150ml (½ cup + 1 tbsp + 2 tsp) sesame oil

Two of my good friends, Sue McLeary and Barbara Horne, took my recipe for a whole-baked salmon, combined it with a recipe for a marinade from Peter Gordon and came up with this. I never go back to my original recipe.

Method

With a large knife, cut 3 diagonal slashes into each side of fish, cutting nearly to the bone.

Place salmon in a deep dish and pour over two-thirds of marinade. Rub marinade into body cavity, cuts and skin.

Leave to marinate in refrigerator for at least 3 hours, turning salmon over and rubbing in marinade after each hour.

Position rack in the centre of oven. Preheat oven to 250°C.

Place salmon on a diagonal in a low-sided roasting tray. For ease of moving cooked salmon, I always place a Teflon sheet on the tray first. If head or tail hangs over side then slightly curve salmon.

Place in oven and cook for 35–40 minutes, or until a metal skewer poked into thickest part of salmon and left for a few minutes comes out piping hot. A 2kg salmon will take 27 minutes to cook.

Remove roasting tray from oven and, using 2 spatulas or by lifting the Teflon sheet, transfer salmon to a serving platter. Slide Teflon sheet out from under the salmon.

Place remaining marinade in a small saucepan and bring to the boil. Strain through a sieve and serve with salmon. Garnish with lime halves.

To Make Soy, Star Anise and Ginger Marinade

Combine all ingredients in a medium-sized bowl.

Roast Turkey Stuffed with Garlic Sourdough

Serves 10

600g (1) sourdough loaf (crusts removed)

1 x 3.5kg turkey (washed and dried)

130ml Garlic Oil

flaky sea salt and freshly ground black pepper

250ml (1 cup) cream

250ml (1 cup) turkey or chicken stock

leaves from 1 sprig rosemary (roughly chopped)

15ml (1 tbsp) balsamic vinegar, or to taste

Garlic Oil – Makes 130ml

12 cloves Roasted Garlic (see page 149)

90ml (6 tbsp) olive oil

leaves from 1 sprig rosemary, roughly chopped

As the stuffing doesn't have egg in it, the turkey can be stuffed up to two days ahead. This version of roast turkey allows you to serve traditional Christmas fare of turkey, in a non-traditional way with dishes such as Asparagus with Anchovies (see page 92) and Potato and Pancetta Gratin (see page 93).

Method

Preheat oven to 190°C.

Cut sourdough loaf into 12–16 chunky pieces and place in a large bowl.

Using a pastry brush, liberally brush the inside cavities of the turkey with Garlic Oil and pour remainder over sourdough.

Mix sourdough and oil to combine well and ensure sourdough has absorbed all the oil.

Season sourdough generously with salt and pepper. Stuff centre and neck cavities of turkey with sourdough stuffing.

Fold wing tips onto back of turkey and secure legs with cotton twine. Place in a large roasting tray and brush with cream.

Adjust oven to 180°C and roast turkey for 30 minutes. Baste again with cream and continue to do so every 20–30 minutes.

Reduce oven temperature to 160°C and roast turkey for a further 1½–2 hours until juices run clear and turkey is cooked.

Remove turkey from roasting tray to another warmed roasting tray and leave to rest covered in aluminium foil for 20 minutes.

Place roasting tray with turkey juices over a medium heat and pour in stock. Stir to combine and remove all baked-on bits off the base of tray. Bring to the boil and simmer to reduce by one-third.

Season jus to taste with salt, pepper and balsamic vinegar.

Carve turkey and serve immediately accompanied with the jus.

To Make Garlic Oil

Squeeze pulp from Roasted Garlic into a small bowl. Mash with a fork, add oil and rosemary and combine.

Fillet of Beef, Bourguignon-style

Serves 8–10

1 (1.2–1.5kg) beef fillet (trimmed)

200g (3 medium) tomatoes

45ml (3 tbsp) olive oil

260–275g (14–16) pearl onions (peeled)

60–75g (16) whole cloves garlic

135g pancetta (diced)

10g dried porcini mushrooms (soaked in 75ml boiling water to rehydrate)

200–230g (16) button mushrooms (stalks trimmed)

375ml (1½ cups) pinot noir

250ml (1 cup) beef stock

1 sprig sage

1 sprig rosemary

2 bay leaves

¼ tsp freshly ground black pepper

½ tsp flaky sea salt

This is a satisfying winter way to cook a beef fillet. You achieve a perfectly cooked beef fillet and an extraordinarily tasty sauce in an all-in-one casserole. I make this recipe in a Le Creuset casserole, a heavy cast-iron casserole which can go on the stove top. Alternatively, use a heavy-based frying pan with a tight-fitting lid. Serve with Garlic Mashed Potatoes with Thyme Crumbs (see page 85).

Method

Secure beef tail (the thin end of the beef fillet) with cotton twine underneath to ensure beef is of even thickness. Tie 8 pieces of twine firmly around fillet at regular intervals. This helps to produce even-shaped steaks once beef is cooked and cut.

Using a sharp knife, put 2 small, shallow cuts in a cross-shape on base of each tomato. Place tomatoes in a bowl and cover with boiling water. Leave to sit for 1–2 minutes. Remove from water and peel skin away from flesh. Cut tomatoes in quarters and deseed. Set aside flesh and discard seeds.

Pour 2 tablespoons of oil into a large, heavy-based frying pan or Le Creuset casserole. Place over a high temperature until hot.

Add beef to frying pan and sear on all sides until well browned.

Remove beef from pan and set aside while you brown the vegetables.

Lower heat to medium-low. Add half the remaining oil, onions and garlic. Cook until onions are golden brown and beginning to soften.

Add pancetta and cook for 2–3 minutes or until golden brown.

Drain porcini and reserve soaking liquid.

Add remaining oil, button mushrooms and porcini to pan and cook for 2–3 minutes until soft. Drain any excess oil.

Add tomatoes, wine, stock, reserved porcini soaking liquid, herbs, pepper and salt.

Stir to combine and bring liquid slowly to the boil.

Return beef to pan and spoon cooking juices all over. Cover pan with a tight-fitting lid.

Return liquid to the boil, lower heat and simmer for approximately 15 minutes or until beef is medium-rare.

Remove beef from pan and leave to rest in a warmed roasting tray covered with a tea towel. While beef is resting, continue to simmer liquid until it is reduced by one-third.

To serve, cut beef between twine into 8–10 even-sized steaks. Remove twine.

Pour some of cooking juices over steak, and remaining juice and vegetables around the plate.

Photograph on following page: Fillet of Beef, Bourguignon-style

Rosemary and Fennel Seed Roast Leg of Pork with Apple Shallot Sauce

Serves 16–20

6–6.5kg leg of pork (skin on)

100ml Rosemary and Fennel Seed Paste

flaky sea salt

1l (4 cups) chicken stock

440ml (1¾ cups) dry white wine

Apple Shallot Sauce (see page 150)

Pancetta and Venison Sausage Stuffing (see page 64)

Rosemary and Fennel Seed Paste – Makes 100ml

8 cloves garlic (peeled and any green shoots removed)

2 tsp finely chopped rosemary leaves

1 tbsp fennel seeds

1 tbsp flaky sea salt

1 tsp freshly ground black pepper

65ml (¼ cup) olive oil

This is a dish which will be well received at a family and friends' celebration. The aroma wafting through the house will get everyone's appetite going and the cook can feel relaxed knowing the sauce is made ahead. The fennel and rosemary are very complementary flavours with pork but also aid the digestion. Order ahead from your butcher to ensure premium pork.

Method

Using a sharp knife, score pork skin by making lines at 2cm intervals across the pork. Cut the lines to a depth of 1cm.

Make deep pockets in pork by inserting paring knife into every second score to a 5cm depth and repeat until there are three rows of pockets on top side of pork and randomly positioned pockets on underside.

Squeeze or poke Rosemary and Fennel Seed Paste into pockets and rub the remaining paste on top of skin and underside of pork.

Place pork in a large roasting pan, cover tightly with plastic wrap and refrigerate for 12–24 hours so that the paste flavours marinate the meat.

Remove pork from refrigerator 2 hours before cooking, and leave in a cool place.

Preheat oven to 200°C.

Uncover pork. Sprinkle with extra salt. Add stock and wine to pan. Place in oven and cook for 30 minutes.

Reduce oven temperature to 180°C and cook pork for a further 2–2½ hours, or until juices are beginning to run clear.

Turn oven up to 200°C and cook for a further 20–30 minutes to crisp up skin to make crackling. The skin should be crisp and a deep, nutty brown colour.

Photograph on previous page: Rosemary and Fennel Seed Roast Leg of Pork with Apple Shallot Sauce (see page 150)
Pancetta and Venison Sausage Stuffing (see page 64)

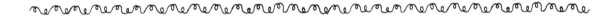

To test if pork is cooked, insert a skewer
or knife into the thickest part of leg and if
juices run clear when removed, it is cooked.

Remove pork from oven and rest pork for
30–45 minutes away from heat, covered
tightly in several sheets of aluminium foil.

Serve with Apple Shallot Sauce (see page
150) and Pancetta and Venison Sausage
Stuffing (see page 64).

To Make Rosemary and Fennel Seed Paste
Place all ingredients in the bowl of a small
food processor fitted with a metal blade and
process to a runny paste. Alternatively, place
ingredients in a mortar and pound together
with a pestle. Store in refrigerator until
ready to use.

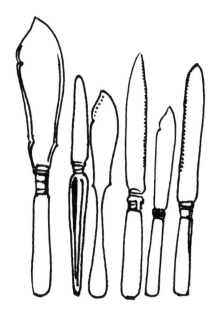

Pancetta and Venison Sausage Stuffing

Makes 11–13 serves

50g (5 tbsp) unsalted butter	1 tbsp finely chopped rosemary	255–300g (11–13) rindless bacon rashers
100g (5–6) shallots (finely chopped)	1 tbsp finely chopped sage	baking spray or melted butter for greasing tray
120g pancetta (diced)	1 tsp finely chopped thyme	
175g (8 cocktail-sized) venison sausages (grilled, cut lengthways into quarters and cubed)	1 preserved lemon (remove pulp and discard, rinse rind and finely dice)	
150g (4–6 thick slices) sourdough bread (crust removed and cut into 2cm dice)	1½ tsp flaky sea salt	
	½ tsp freshly ground black pepper	

This is a very tasty add-on to Rosemary and Fennel Seed Roast Leg of Pork (see page 62) but also serve as you would a meat loaf, even though it is not as firm as a meat loaf.

Method

In a heavy-based frying pan, melt butter over a medium heat. Add shallots and cook for 1–2 minutes, or until shallots are soft.

Add pancetta and cook a further 2–3 minutes until pancetta is just starting to colour. Add sausages and stir through. Add bread and lightly toss until well combined. Continue to toss gently for 1–2 minutes until bread is well coated in butter.

Transfer to a bowl and stir in herbs, preserved lemon, salt and pepper. Cool.

Lay bacon rashers out on a large piece of plastic wrap. Place stuffing down the centre of bacon rashers and wrap bacon around stuffing. Wrap plastic wrap as firmly as possible around stuffing.

Rest in refrigerator for at least 2 hours, or overnight.

Preheat oven to 180°C.

Remove plastic wrap from stuffing. Grease a roasting tray with baking spray or melted butter.

Place stuffing on roasting tray, place in oven and roast for 40–45 minutes or until firm and bacon is crisp. Remove from oven and serve.

Beef Wellington with Red Wine and Balsamic Sauce

Makes 10–12 serves

1.5kg (1) beef fillet (trimmed of all silver skin – your butcher will do this for you)

15ml (1 tbsp) olive oil

120g Chicken Liver Pâté (see page 19)

Dry-roasted Mushrooms

freshly ground black pepper

flour for dusting bench

660g puff pastry (buy the most buttery puff pastry you can find)

1 egg white (lightly beaten)

egg wash (1 lightly beaten egg yolk mixed with 1 tbsp water)

Red Wine and Balsamic Sauce (see page 150)

Dry-roasted Mushrooms

500g large button mushrooms (trimmed and finely chopped)

An oldie but a goodie. This is the version we use at Ruth Pretty Catering developed so that the Beef Wellington can be prepared up to two days ahead. Because it is a rich dish, accompaniments do not need to be lavish or large. Enjoy with Herbed New Potatoes with Peas (see page 86) and freshly cooked beans or asparagus.

Method

Preheat oven to 200°C.

Brush beef fillet with oil. Preheat a heavy-based frying pan or flat grill plate to hot. Sear beef well on all sides. Remove from pan, place on a low-sided baking tray and cook in oven for 20 minutes or until beef is medium-rare.

Remove from oven and cool completely.

Spread entire fillet with pâté. Sprinkle Dry-roasted Mushrooms over pâté and press lightly to help them stick. Grind black pepper over mushroom layer.

Lightly dust bench with flour. Roll pastry into a rectangle (approximately 45 x 26cm, 3–4mm thickness).

Brush pastry lightly with egg white. (Egg white prevents pastry becoming soggy and also seals joins.)

Place fillet on pastry 10cm in from long edge. Lift pastry over fillet to completely cover. Trim pastry ends by cutting on an angle …

... Beef Wellington with Red Wine and Balsamic Sauce

…Open pastry end and fold the top piece of pastry under the beef with an envelope-fold. Bring the bottom piece of pastry up, envelope-fold and press onto pastry top.

Turn whole fillet over so top becomes bottom and all pastry joins are underneath. Decorate top of Beef Wellington as desired. For example, cut scraps of pastry into leaf shapes. Adhere to pastry case with egg white.

Rest Beef Wellington in refrigerator for a minimum of 30 minutes or up to 2 days.

Preheat oven to 220°C.

Brush Beef Wellington with egg wash, place in oven and bake for 20–25 minutes until pastry is cooked through and golden brown all over.

Remove from oven and leave to rest for 10 minutes.

Strain shallots and garlic from Red Wine and Balsamic Sauce and reserve for another use. Slice Beef Wellington into 10–12 serves and drizzle with sauce.

To Make Dry-roasted Mushrooms
Preheat oven to 200°C.

Place mushrooms on a cold roasting tray and cook for 15–20 minutes until mushrooms are soft and dry. Cool.

Duck Breast with Tawari Honey and Pinot Noir Lavender Sauce

Serves 8

1.4–1.5kg (8) boneless duck breasts with skin on

175ml (½ cup + 3 tbsp + 1 tsp) Tawari Honey and Lavender Marinade

375ml (1½ cups) Tawari Honey and Pinot Noir Lavender Sauce (see page 145)

Tawari Honey and Lavender Marinade – Makes 175ml

125ml (½ cup) olive oil

30ml (2 tbsp) Tawari honey, or another light floral honey

2 tbsp finely chopped shallots

4 tsp finely chopped fresh lavender leaves or 1 tsp dried culinary lavender

flowers. Use English varieties such as *Lavandula Angustifolia* or *Lavandula Intermedia*

2 tsp black peppercorns

2 tsp mustard seeds

2 tsp coriander seeds

This recipe calls for the skin to be removed from the duck breasts. To many people this may seem like sacrilege, in which case proceed with the skin on, but I enjoy the lightness of the duck with the skin removed. This is an elegant main course and should be served with Potatoes Roasted in Duck Fat (see page 81).

Method

Remove duck skin from breasts and reserve for Rendered Duck Fat (see page 81).

Place duck breasts in a low-sided ceramic baking dish. Pour marinade over duck and turn duck in marinade to coat.

Cover with plastic wrap and leave to marinate overnight in refrigerator or for 1 hour at room temperature.

Preheat oven to 220°C.

Heat a heavy-based frying pan to hot. Remove duck from marinade and rub off excess marinade. Add duck breasts to pan, a few at a time, and quickly brown each side. Transfer duck to a low-sided roasting tray, place in oven and roast for 5–7 minutes, or until cooked medium-rare.

Transfer duck to a warmed plate, cover with a heavy tea towel and leave to rest for 5 minutes.

Slice duck across the grain and serve drizzled with Tawari Honey and Pinot Noir Lavender Sauce.

To Make Tawari Honey and Lavender Marinade

Combine all marinade ingredients.

Barbecued Seafood Salad with Lemon Basil Dressing

Serves 4

16 scampi tails (thawed) or 16 large prawns (heads removed)

400g (16) pieces fresh, firm fish, such as groper (hapuka), blue cod or tuna (cut into 20–25g portions)

16 scallops (rinsed and cleaned)

440ml Lemon Basil Marinade

½ preserved lemon (remove and discard pulp, rinse rind and slice)

15ml (1 tbsp) olive oil

flaky sea salt and freshly ground black pepper

24 caperberries

8 large handfuls prepared salad greens

Lemon Basil Marinade – Makes 440ml

250ml (1 cup) extra virgin olive oil

160ml (½ cup + 2 tbsp + 1 tsp) lemon juice (juice of 5–6 lemons)

16g (4) cloves garlic (smashed)

2 tbsp sliced basil leaves

flaky sea salt and freshly ground black pepper

This is a special occasion summer dish designed to be enjoyed outside. If you wish, accompany with little new potatoes also dressed with the Lemon Basil Dressing.

Method

Butterfly scampi tails by cutting lengthways through the outside shell and place in a bowl. Place fish in another bowl and scallops in another bowl.

Pour half Lemon Basil Marinade over each bowl of seafood so as to just cover and leave at room temperature for 15–20 minutes.

To make Lemon Basil Dressing, add preserved lemon to remaining half of Lemon Basil Marinade.

Heat barbecue flat plate to medium-hot.

Drain marinade from seafood and discard liquid.

Brush barbecue plate with olive oil. Add scampi tails, placing butterflied side onto barbecue. Cook for 3–4 minutes or until just cooked through.

Add fish pieces and cook for 2–3 minutes each side. Add scallops and sear for 1–2 minutes each side.

As seafood cooks, remove it from barbecue and place it in a large, low-sided bowl so that it sits in a single layer. Season with salt and pepper.

Place caperberries on barbecue for 1–2 minutes to just warm through.

Divide salad greens evenly between 4 plates, or place on a platter. Place seafood on salad greens and drizzle with Lemon Basil Dressing. Garnish with caperberries and serve immediately.

To Make Lemon Basil Marinade

In a small bowl combine olive oil, lemon juice, garlic and basil and season to taste. Set aside for at least 20–30 minutes, or overnight, for flavours to infuse.

Discard garlic cloves before using.

four

Vegetables & Salads

Your friends and family will appreciate big servings of all the recipes in Vegetables & Salads. Many of these dishes can be the focus of a meal, part of an antipasto or an entrée before the main course.

Buttercrunch, Avocado and Hazelnut Salad with Hazelnut Vinaigrette

Serves 6

1 buttercrunch lettuce
(washed and preferably
spun in a salad spinner)

1 avocado (peeled and
sliced)

50g hazelnuts (lightly
roasted, roughly peeled
and coarsely chopped)

20–25 basil leaves
(roughly torn)

2 lemons (cut into wedges)
(optional)

Hazelnut Vinaigrette

50ml (3 tbsp + 1 tsp)
hazelnut oil

5 ml (1 tsp) balsamic
vinegar

flaky sea salt and freshly
ground black pepper

Aim for very fresh, locally grown hazelnuts
and prepare this quick-to-put-together
salad as you are about to serve. Sometimes
I use white balsamic condiment instead of
balsamic vinegar to make a more unique-
flavoured dressing.

Method

Place Hazelnut Vinaigrette ingredients in a
low-sided salad bowl and whisk to combine.

Gently tear lettuce and place lettuce,
avocado, hazelnuts and basil leaves into
salad bowl on top of dressing. Gently toss
to combine. Accompany each serve with
a lemon wedge, if you wish.

Iceberg Salad from La Rioja

Serves 4	La Rioja Vinaigrette – Makes 195ml
1 clove garlic (halved lengthways)	45ml (3 tbsp) Spanish sherry vinegar
100g (½–1) iceberg lettuce (outer leaves and core removed)	30ml (2 tbsp) Spanish red wine vinegar
30g (⅓–½) red onion (halved and thinly sliced)	60ml (4 tbsp) olive oil
45–60ml (3–4 tbsp) La Rioja Vinaigrette	60ml (4 tbsp) Spanish extra virgin olive oil
	flaky sea salt and freshly ground black pepper

I first sampled this traditional Spanish salad at Marques de Riscal, an extraordinary vineyard and winery in La Rioja, Spain. Lunch had been cooked by a local woman who disappeared before I could thank her. No matter when I serve this salad I am always asked for the recipe. It is so simple and obvious that I am afraid to tell people.

Method

Rub garlic around the inside of a salad bowl until garlic begins to break. (I like to use a wooden salad bowl.) Leave broken garlic in salad bowl.

Wash and drain lettuce. Roll lettuce leaves tightly and thinly slice.

Place lettuce and onion in salad bowl and, just prior to serving, pour vinaigrette over lettuce and onion. Toss together and serve immediately.

Any remaining vinaigrette can be poured into a bottle or jar, covered and refrigerated for 2–3 weeks.

To Make La Rioja Vinaigrette

Into a small bowl pour vinegars and oils and whisk to form an emulsion. Season to taste with salt and pepper.

Chargrilled Zucchini with Mint Raita

Serves 8

800g (6) zucchini (cut lengthways into 5mm thick slices)

100ml Lemon-infused Olive Oil (see page 153)

Mint Raita – Makes 130ml

125ml (½ cup) Greek-style yoghurt

¼ tsp garam masala

¼ tsp black mustard seeds (toasted and ground)

1 tsp finely grated lemon zest

3 tbsp firmly packed sliced mint

flaky sea salt and freshly ground black pepper

Serve as a starter when zucchini are at their peak, as part of a vegetable antipasto or as an accompaniment to barbecue meats. Chargrilled Zucchini with Mint Raita is also very good stuffed into pita breads with barbecued meats.

Method

Preheat chargrill plate to medium-hot.

Into a large bowl place zucchini and lemon oil and toss to coat.

Place zucchini onto preheated chargrill and grill for 2–3 minutes on each side, moving it once on each side to achieve criss-cross grill marks and until zucchini is just cooked and lightly coloured.

Remove zucchini from chargrill and serve with Mint Raita.

Serve warm.

To Make Mint Raita

Combine all ingredients in a bowl.

Photograph on following page: Chargrilled Zucchini with Mint Raita

Tomato and Toasted Sourdough Salad

Serves 4–5

1 loaf day-old sourdough bread	¼ tsp freshly ground black pepper
65–85ml (¼–⅓ cup) olive oil	20g (2 tbsp) pine nuts (lightly toasted)
75–90g (2 heads) Roasted Garlic (see page 149)	465–540g (6–8) very ripe tomatoes (cores removed and roughly chopped)
65ml (¼ cup) extra virgin olive oil	9–12 large basil leaves (torn)
30ml (2 tbsp) red wine vinegar	
½ tsp flaky sea salt	

Serve this juicy robust salad with Springfield Roast Chicken (see page 34), as part of a vegetable antipasto, or with barbecued meats. This dish should be made when tomatoes are at their peak to really do it justice.

Method

Cut sourdough loaf in half lengthways and cut off crusts. Break into uneven, bite-sized chunks. (You require around 4 cups.)

Place olive oil in a bowl, add bread and quickly toss together so bread is coated with oil.

Preheat a heavy-based frying pan and cook bread on all sides until crisp and golden brown.

Squeeze pulp from roasted garlic, place in bowl, mash with a fork and add bread to bowl. Toss together so bread is coated with garlic.

Place extra virgin olive oil, vinegar, salt and pepper in a salad bowl and whisk together.

Add bread, pine nuts, tomatoes and basil to bowl and toss together. Season to taste.

Photograph on previous page: Tomato and Toasted Sourdough Salad

Potatoes Roasted in Duck Fat

Serves 6–8

45g (3 tbsp) Rendered Duck Fat

650–750g (6–8 medium) starchy potatoes (peeled and cut into 3–4 wedge-shaped pieces)

flaky sea salt and freshly ground black pepper

Rendered Duck Fat – Makes 100–130g

290–400g duck skin and fat (from 4 duck breasts you may get this amount. When you prepare duck breasts trim off any flaps of skin. The skin will have fat attached. In the duck recipe on page 68 the recipe calls for all skin to be removed from duck breasts)

The truly great by-product of cooking duck is its fat. Duck fat is available to buy at some specialty shops. Once you have eaten potatoes roasted in duck fat it is difficult to go back. A simple secret to perfect roast potatoes is not to turn them during their cooking time.

Method

Preheat oven to 200°C.

Place duck fat in a roasting pan and place in oven for 5 minutes until melted and sizzling.

Thoroughly dry potatoes with a tea towel or paper towels and place in roasting pan. Toss potatoes in hot duck fat. Sprinkle with salt and pepper. Return to oven and cook for 30–45 minutes until potatoes are cooked, golden in colour and crisp.

Remove pan from oven and, using a slice or metal scraper, transfer potatoes from pan to a warmed serving bowl.

Sprinkle with salt and serve immediately.

To Make Rendered Duck Fat

Preheat oven to 150°C.

Place skin and fat in a small ovenproof dish with a lid on.

Place dish in oven and leave to cook for 1 hour. Stir once or twice during the cooking time.

Remove from oven and strain rendered fat through a fine sieve into a small bowl. Discard solids.

Place fat in refrigerator to harden. Solid, very clean, white duck fat should remain.

Store covered in refrigerator for up to 1 week, or in the freezer for up to 3 months.

Pear, Celery and Walnut Salad with Honey Vinaigrette

Serves 6–8

2 pears (firm but juicy variety such as Red Comice or Doyenne du Comice, quartered, cored and thinly sliced)

juice of ½ lemon

95g (¾ cup) walnuts (toasted)

3 celery stalks with leaves (preferably from heart, chopped)

6–8 large handfuls of baby salad greens, combined with assorted soft herb leaves, such as chervil, Italian parsley, chives and salad burnet

Honey Vinaigrette

1 tsp honey

30ml (2 tbsp) extra virgin olive oil

30ml (2 tbsp) walnut oil

15ml (1 tbsp) balsamic vinegar

flaky sea salt and freshly ground pepper to taste

This is my favourite winter salad. I often enjoy this salad as the focus of a meal with a piece of cheese, such as a creamy blue or brie-style, but it is also really good with roast chicken. Its beauty does rely on fresh walnuts, so buy locally grown ones.

Method

Place pears in a small bowl with lemon juice and toss together.

Combine Honey Vinaigrette ingredients in a salad bowl.

Place walnuts, celery and pears into salad bowl, on top of Honey Vinaigrette, then place salad greens and herb leaves on top. Toss lightly to combine ingredients.

Serve immediately.

1.

2.

3.

Garlic Mashed Potatoes
with Thyme Crumbs

Serves 8

baking spray or melted butter for greasing dish

1kg potatoes (preferably Agria, peeled)

60ml (4 tbsp) olive oil

1 egg yolk (lightly beaten)

pulp from 20 cloves Roasted Garlic (see page 149)

freshly ground nutmeg

Thyme Crumbs

flaky sea salt and freshly ground black pepper

20g (2 tbsp) butter

15ml (1 tbsp) olive oil

35g (¼) onion (finely diced)

75g (1 cup) fresh breadcrumbs

1 tsp thyme (finely chopped)

This is a useful mashed potato dish as it can be prepared up to two days in advance and then baked as required. The egg yolk in the recipe prevents the reheated mashed potato from becoming stodgy.

Method

Grease a 30 x 20cm ovenproof gratin dish, or similar, with baking spray or melted butter.

Cut potatoes into pieces and place in a steamer, set over a medium heat and cook until soft. (Steaming the potatoes as opposed to boiling them will prevent them from becoming watery.) Place in a bowl and mash with a potato masher.

Add oil followed by egg yolk, garlic and nutmeg, salt and pepper to taste and beat together.

Place into prepared gratin dish. Scatter Thyme Crumbs on top of potato. Store in refrigerator for up to 2 days or proceed to next step.

When ready to bake, preheat oven to 150°C. Place gratin dish in oven and bake for 30–40 minutes or until top is golden brown and potatoes are hot. Serve immediately.

To Make Thyme Crumbs

Place butter and olive oil in a small saucepan over a low heat and melt butter. Add onion and cook for 3–4 minutes or until onion is soft.

Add breadcrumbs and cook, stirring frequently, until breadcrumbs just begin to colour. Add thyme and a grind of black pepper and combine.

1. Garlic Mashed Potatoes with Thyme Crumbs   2. Herbed New Potatoes with Peas (see page 86)   3. Herbed Lemon Orzo Salad (see page 87)

Herbed New Potatoes with Peas

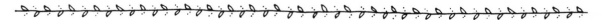

Serves 8–10

50g (5 tbsp) unsalted butter	140g sugar snap peas (topped and tailed)
1kg (24–30) small waxy potatoes (washed but not peeled)	1 tbsp finely chopped chervil
2 tsp flaky sea salt	1 tbsp finely chopped dill
¼ tsp freshly ground black pepper	1 tbsp finely sliced chives
130g (1 cup) frozen or fresh peas (blanched)	

Serve this potato dish with roast beef, lamb or grilled fish but in particular I enjoy it with Beef Wellington with Red Wine and Balsamic Sauce (see page 65). You need a heavy-based casserole dish to achieve browned butter and smoky flavour of the dish.

Method

Place butter in a medium-sized, heavy-based casserole dish with a tight-fitting lid. Place over a medium-low heat to melt butter.

Add potatoes, salt and pepper and toss well to coat potatoes in butter.

Cover casserole and cook over medium-low heat for 25–30 minutes without lifting lid until potatoes are fork-tender. Shake casserole occasionally to prevent potatoes on bottom from burning. (A SimmerMat is extremely useful in cooking this dish.)

Once cooked, turn off heat, add peas and sugar snap peas and leave to steam for a further 5 minutes.

Add herbs and gently shake saucepan from side to side to combine ingredients.

Serve immediately.

Alternative Method of Cooking

To achieve a similar but not quite as tasty result, place covered casserole or saucepan in an oven preheated to 190°C and cook for 40–50 minutes until potatoes are fork-tender and beginning to brown.

Herbed Lemon Orzo Salad

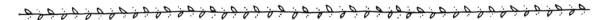

Serves 8

½ tsp flaky sea salt

320g (1½ cups) orzo

finely grated zest of
3 lemons

15ml (1 tbsp) extra virgin
olive oil

45ml (3 tbsp) freshly
squeezed lemon juice

⅓ cup roughly chopped
chives

⅓ cup chopped Italian
parsley leaves

⅓ cup mint leaves (large
leaves torn in half)

flaky sea salt and freshly
ground black pepper

Orzo is rice-shaped pasta sometimes
labelled riso or rizo. This is a useful do-ahead
salad to take to a barbecue, or to serve at
your own barbecue or buffet as the starch
accompaniment.

Method

Three-quarters fill a heavy-based large
saucepan with water and bring to the boil.

Add salt and orzo. Stir and bring back to the
boil. Reduce heat and simmer uncovered for
10–12 minutes or until orzo is al dente.

Drain orzo and while it is warm add lemon
zest, oil, lemon juice, chives, parsley and
mint. Season to taste and serve while it is
warm. Alternatively cool and refrigerate
salad to serve cold.

Green Beans with Lemon-infused Olive Oil

Serves 10

½ tsp flaky sea salt

750g green beans

15ml (1 tbsp) Lemon-infused Olive Oil (see page 153)

flaky sea salt and freshly ground black pepper

When beans are at their best the simplest preparation wins out. Serve with everything. If beans are the flat variety, I like to slice them using an old-fashioned bean slicer so they are as thin as spaghetti. If they are round beans just trim off the ends.

Method

Bring a large saucepan of lightly salted water to the boil. Add salt and plunge beans into water. Cook uncovered, until just past al dente. Drain.

If you are not serving beans immediately, line a bowl with a cold wet tea towel and place hot, undressed but drained beans into the bowl. Bring the edges of the tea towel up to cover beans. Beans will remain green and hot for up to 30 minutes held this way.

Just before serving, drizzle with Lemon-infused Olive Oil and add salt and pepper to taste. Gently toss together.

1.

2.

3.

Vegetable Salad with Orange, Cumin and Mint Vinaigrette

Serves 6–8

½ tsp flaky sea salt

150g broccoli florets (washed)

150g (5–7) baby carrots (scraped and halved) or 150g carrots (peeled and julienned)

150g (1–2) yellow zucchini (cut into batons)

150g (1–2) green zucchini (cut into batons)

100g (1) celery heart (leaves torn and stalks chopped)

130ml Orange, Cumin and Mint Vinaigrette (see page 149)

You can exchange any of the vegetables in this colourful crunchy salad with seasonal vegetables, but always retain the celery.

Method

Bring a large saucepan of water to the boil. Add salt. Place broccoli in a sieve which will fit into the saucepan and submerge in the water. Cook for 2 minutes or until broccoli is bright green. Remove sieve from saucepan and refresh broccoli under cold running water. Repeat cooking process with carrots and zucchini, cooking carrots for 3 minutes and zucchini for 2 minutes, refreshing each vegetable under cold running water. Lay vegetables out on a tea towel and pat dry.

In a large bowl combine vegetables with celery leaves and stalks.

Pour Orange, Cumin and Mint Vinaigrette over vegetables and toss to coat.

Serve at room temperature.

1. Vegetable Salad with Orange, Cumin and Mint Vinaigrette   2. Asparagus with Anchovies (see page 92)   3. Potato and Pancetta Gratin (see page 93)

Asparagus with Anchovies

Serves 6–8

60ml (4 tbsp) olive oil

40g (4 tbsp) unsalted butter

680–720g (40) thin asparagus (washed and pinged)

20g (6) anchovies (rinsed and thinly sliced)

45ml (3 tbsp) lemon juice

¼ cup finely chopped Italian parsley

flaky sea salt and freshly ground black pepper

1½ cups Croutons

Croutons – Makes 1½ cups

2 slices thick white toast bread

canola oil for frying

flaky sea salt

For guests who say they don't like anchovies change the title of this dish because all my anti-anchovy friends love it. It is tasty as a first course, but also a lovely vegetable accompaniment to simple roast and grilled meats. To ping asparagus, exert gentle pressure at the stalk end until the woody end snaps off, leaving the tender part of the spear and tip. Enjoy this dish with Roast Turkey Stuffed with Garlic Sourdough (see page 56).

Method

In a heavy-based frying pan over a medium heat, place olive oil and butter and cook until butter is melted. Add asparagus and anchovies and cook for 3–4 minutes until asparagus is just tender.

Remove asparagus with anchovies from pan and place on a platter.

Add lemon juice, parsley and seasoning to taste to pan juices. Drizzle pan juices over asparagus.

Scatter Croutons over the top and serve while asparagus is still warm.

To Make Croutons

Using an electric or serrated-edged knife remove crusts from bread and cut bread into even-sized 1–1.5cm cubes.

Pour oil to a 5mm depth into a heavy-based frying pan and heat until hot enough for frying.

Drop bread cubes into oil and toss in hot oil for 1–2 minutes until golden brown and crisp.

Using a slotted spoon quickly remove bread cubes from pan and place onto paper towels to absorb excess oil.

While still hot, sprinkle with salt and toss to fully coat. Cool.

Store in an airtight container until needed.

Potato and Pancetta Gratin

Serves 6–8

850g (6) medium-sized potatoes (preferably Agrias, peeled)

30ml (2 tbsp) olive oil

100g pancetta (diced)

20g (5) cloves garlic (thinly sliced)

3 tbsp roughly chopped rosemary or sage leaves

280ml (1 cup + 2 tbsp + 2 tsp) chicken stock

flaky sea salt and freshly ground black pepper

50g (½ cup + 3 tbsp) finely grated Parmesan

This potato dish is a tasty accompaniment to Roast Turkey Stuffed with Garlic Sourdough (see page 56) and easy on the cook as the prepared ingredients can be taken from the refrigerator, assembled in the baking dish, and cooked while the turkey is resting.

Method

Preheat oven to 190°C.

Slice each potato lengthways down the centre and place in a large bowl.

Heat oil in a small frying pan over a medium heat. Add pancetta and cook for 2–3 minutes until it begins to colour. Add garlic and herbs and cook for a further 2 minutes but do not brown.

Remove from heat and sprinkle pancetta mixture over potatoes. Add stock, salt and pepper and, with your hands, gently toss mixture together.

Place mixture into a 29 x 20cm oval gratin dish or similar (aim for a baking dish with a 1–1.3 litre capacity). Cover with aluminium foil, place in oven and bake for 40–50 minutes, or until potatoes are tender.

Remove aluminium foil, and, using a spoon, collect juices surrounding potatoes and drizzle over potatoes. Sprinkle with Parmesan and cook for a further 10–12 minutes or until golden brown.

Serve immediately.

five

Desserts

At home with friends and family, everyone saves
a little bit of space for dessert. Indeed, they have a
separate dessert compartment in their stomachs.
Be sure to satisfy them with one of my favourites.

Amaretto Panna Cotta

Serves 8

500ml (2 cups) milk

16g (2 tbsp) gelatine powder

500ml (2 cups) cream

105g (½ cup) castor sugar

75ml (5 tbsp) amaretto

Panna cotta is a soft, sweet whisper of a dessert and this version incorporates the nutty flavour of amaretto, the almond liqueur known as the liqueur of love.

Method

Place 125ml (½ cup) of the milk in a bowl and sprinkle with gelatine. Stir to combine and leave for 5 minutes or until gelatine has softened and absorbed the milk.

Pour remaining milk and cream into a heavy-based saucepan and place over a medium heat. Add castor sugar and stir until sugar is dissolved.

Bring mixture to the boil, remove from heat and let it sit for 2 minutes so it is not at boiling temperature when it is mixed with gelatine. Add softened gelatine and stir until gelatine is dissolved. Strain mixture through a fine sieve and, very importantly, cool completely.

Stir in amaretto and pour into a 1 litre serving bowl or jelly mould.

Chill panna cotta for at least 4 hours or overnight until set.

Serve from bowl or, if a jelly mould, unmould onto a platter. Accompany with berries, macerated tamarillos, orange slices, poached pears, with cool Chocolate Sauce (see page 144) or with chilled glasses of amaretto.

Sticky Banana Puddings with Caramel Sauce

Serves 10

baking spray or melted butter for greasing dishes	1 tsp vanilla extract or essence
Caramel Sauce (see page 144)	105g (¾ cup) high-grade flour
530–580g (3) ripe bananas (skin on)	1½ tsp baking powder
	¼ tsp salt
180g unsalted butter (diced and at room temperature)	2–3 Crunchie bars (coarsely broken into chunks) (optional)
180g (¾ cup + 3 tbsp) sugar	whipped cream (optional)
3 eggs	

My friend Karen Holder enjoyed this wintry pudding so much at Sweet Basil restaurant in Hong Kong she begged the chef for the recipe, knowing I would love it. These puddings can be baked a day ahead and reheated in the oven at 150°C for around 15 minutes with the puddings covered in a water bath. They can also be frozen unbaked, and baked from frozen, allowing 2–3 minutes additional cooking time.

Method

Grease 10 x 125ml soufflé dishes, dariole moulds or ovenproof espresso cups with baking spray or melted butter. Pour enough Caramel Sauce into each mould to make a caramel base 1.5cm deep. Reserve remaining Caramel Sauce for serving with puddings.

Preheat oven to 200°C.

Place bananas in their skins onto a low-sided baking tray and roast for 10 minutes or until mushy. Cool. Remove flesh from skins and discard skins.

Place butter and sugar in a bowl and beat until smooth and creamy. Add eggs one at a time, beating well after each addition.

Add banana flesh and vanilla and mix until combined.

Sift flour, baking powder and salt into mixture and fold in.

Spoon batter into moulds on top of Caramel Sauce base.

Cover each mould with aluminium foil and place in a roasting dish. To allow puddings to steam in oven, pour hot water to 2–3cm

Springfield Limoncello

Makes 1 x 700ml bottle

375g (4) lemons (washed and chopped into large chunks, with peel on)

420g (2 cups) castor sugar

375ml (1½ cups) vodka

375ml (1½ cups) water

depth (or to come halfway up sides of moulds) into roasting dish and cover entire dish with aluminium foil.

Place in oven and cook for 30 minutes or until pudding feels spongy on top.

Remove from oven and remove aluminium foil.

To Serve

Tip each pudding into the centre of a serving plate, pouring Caramel Sauce in base of mould over top of pudding.

Heat remaining Caramel Sauce.

If you wish, sprinkle each pudding with a tablespoon of Crunchie chunks and accompany with remaining Caramel Sauce and whipped cream.

Italians say that a digestif, designed to aid digestion, helps you to sleep well. This version, inspired by cocktail expert Hayden Wood, is very much a cheat's method of making lemon liqueur but with home-grown lemons it is a very worthy beverage. Serve instead of dessert.

Method

Place lemons and sugar in a large bowl and bruise fruit by squashing with the handle of a rolling pin or a muddler. Add lemon rind, vodka and water to bowl. Stir to dissolve sugar. If sugar does not dissolve easily, leave for 1 hour then stir again. Cover with plastic wrap and allow to infuse for 48 hours at room temperature.

Strain limoncello through a sieve, discarding lemons. Pour liquid, using a funnel, into empty bottle to store.

Place bottle in freezer to chill and to store and serve very chilled as shots.

1.

2.

3.

Zuccotto

Serves 12–15

2 x Vanilla Sponge Cakes (1 x 42 x 29cm rectangle; and 1 x 23cm round or a diameter equivalent to the top of your pudding bowl (see page 102)

65ml (¼ cup) Crème de Framboise (raspberry liqueur)

550g (2½ cups + 2 tbsp) ricotta

1½ tsp vanilla extract or essence

225g (1½ cups) icing sugar

235g (1 cup) mascarpone

250ml (1 cup) cream (lightly whipped)

65g (½ cup) pistachios (roasted and roughly chopped)

65g (½ cup) hazelnuts (roasted, skinned and roughly chopped)

250g (1½ cups) dark chocolate, preferably 70%

(buttons or tablet coarsely chopped)

65g (½ cup) mixed peel (chopped)

240g (2 cups) fresh raspberries or thawed from frozen

Raspberry Sauce (see page 145)

A spectacular dessert for a special occasion, particularly if sliced in front of guests. Can be made up to two days in advance if kept refrigerated. It has been said that leftovers are great at breakfast.

Method

Line a 2.5 litre-capacity pudding bowl with plastic wrap, allowing enough of an overhang to cover top of bowl. Place sponge rectangle onto a large chopping board and, using a pastry cutter, cut a 4.5cm round. With a sharp knife, cut remaining sponge rectangle in half lengthways. Cut each rectangular piece into 3.5cm strips and cut each strip in half to make triangles.

Place 4.5cm round in centre of prepared bowl and line sides with sponge triangles, top side facing up, fitting them together tightly. Fill in any gaps with leftover sponge.

Using a pastry brush, dab Crème de Framboise over the sponge lining the bowl.

Place ricotta, vanilla and sugar in the bowl of a food processor fitted with a metal blade and process until smooth. Add mascarpone and, using pulse button on processor, incorporate mascarpone until smooth.

Transfer to a large bowl. Place cream, nuts, chocolate and mixed peel into ricotta mixture and fold together until incorporated …

... Zuccotto

Vanilla Sponge Cakes

Makes 1 x 42 x 29cm rectangle and 1 x 23cm round

baking spray or melted butter for greasing tray and tin
6 eggs (separated)
210g (1 cup + 1 tbsp) sugar
1½ tsp vanilla extract or essence
¼ tsp salt
105g (¾ cup) high-grade flour
100g (¾ cup) cornflour

... Gently fold in raspberries, trying not to break fruit.

Gently spoon ricotta mixture into sponge-lined bowl, pushing down to remove any air pockets.

Top with the round sponge and cover with overhang of plastic wrap. Refrigerate for at least 8 hours, or overnight.

When ready to serve, remove plastic wrap from top of bowl. To remove Zuccotto from bowl, place a large serving platter over bowl and flip bowl and plate together. Remove bowl and plastic wrap.

Drizzle with Raspberry Sauce and present remainder as accompaniment. If you wish, sit a decorative item, such as a small Christmas bell, on top of the dome shape, or form a decorative knob from sponge off-cuts.

If the sponge cake is to be used in Zuccotto, or for that matter in a trifle, it can be wrapped in plastic wrap and frozen until required.

Method

Preheat oven to 180°C.

Line a 42 x 29cm low-sided baking tray and 23cm round tin with baking paper and lightly grease paper with baking spray or melted butter.

Place egg yolks, 150g (¾ cup) of the sugar and vanilla in a bowl, preferably of an electric mixer, and whisk until thick and pale in colour. Transfer to a clean, large bowl.

Wash and dry mixing bowl and whisk. Place egg whites and salt in the bowl and whisk until soft peaks form. While whisking, slowly add the remaining 60g (6 tbsp) of sugar. Continue whisking until thick and glossy.

Vanilla Bean
Ice Cream

Makes 650ml

295ml (1 cup + 3 tbsp) cream	1 vanilla bean (cut in half lengthways)
295ml (1 cup + 3 tbsp) milk	155ml (½ cup + 2 tbsp + 2 tsp) cream
3 egg yolks (well beaten)	
90g (½ cup + 2 tsp) raw sugar (raw sugar gives the ice cream colour and flavour)	10g (1 tbsp) sugar

Fold egg-white mixture into yolk mixture.

Sieve flour and cornflour together and gradually fold into egg mixture.

Pour two-thirds of mixture into baking tray and remaining third into round cake tin. Gently spread out and smooth the tops.

Place in oven and bake for 12–15 minutes until light golden or until a metal skewer when inserted comes out clean. Transfer cakes to wire racks to cool.

This non-churn ice cream is much creamier and more flavoursome than a commercial variety so is definitely worth the small amount of effort.

Method

Into a saucepan pour first measure of cream and milk. Add egg yolks and raw sugar. Scrape seeds from vanilla bean and add seeds and bean to mixture. Stir to combine.

Place over a medium-low heat, stirring constantly until mixture thickens and coats back of wooden spoon thickly.

Remove from heat, strain to remove vanilla bean and residual strands of egg white. Cool.

Lightly whip second measure of cream with sugar.

Gently fold into custard.*

Pour into freezer-proof container and cover surface of ice cream with plastic wrap.

Cover container so that it is airtight. Freeze for 4 hours or overnight. Store in freezer for up to 1 week.

Diet-be-damned Brownie Ice Cream

Strawberry Sundae

Makes 700ml / Serves 8–10

650ml Vanilla Bean Ice Cream (see page 103), prepared up to final stage*

100g Diet-be-damned Brownie (see page 133. Save the trimmings and break into 2–3cm chunky pieces)

Serves 6

650ml Vanilla Bean Ice Cream (see page 103)

180g (18–24) large ripe strawberries (cut into quarters)

190ml (¾ cup) Chocolate Sauce (see page 144)

People of all ages will love my version of Cookies 'n' Cream. It will be difficult to go back to the supermarket version.

Method

Prepare Vanilla Bean Ice Cream. At the same time that you fold cream into custard base, add brownie and fold through until brownie is evenly distributed and just beginning to break up.

Pour into freezer-proof container and cover surface of ice cream with plastic wrap. Cover container so that it is airtight. Freeze for 4 hours or overnight. Store in freezer for up to 1 week.

Old-fashioned, thick sundae glasses can be found at junk shops or new versions can be bought from kitchenware or gift stores. Strawberries, vanilla ice cream and chocolate sauce is a timeless sundae combination. It seems a simple dessert so you may be surprised by its popularity.

Method

Into each sundae glass place a scoop of Vanilla Bean Ice Cream. Top with 4–5 strawberry quarters. Repeat layers until glass is overflowing.

Pour 2 tablespoons of hot Chocolate Sauce over top allowing it to drizzle down side of glass onto ice cream and strawberries below.

Serve immediately with spoons long enough to reach bottom of glass.

Photograph on following page: Strawberry Sundae

Chocolate Roulade

Serves 8–10

baking spray or melted butter for greasing tin	135g (½ cup + 3 tbsp) castor sugar
135g dark chocolate, preferably 70% (buttons or coarsely chopped tablet)	pinch salt
	Chocolate Mousse (see page 109)
35ml (2 tbsp + 1 tsp) freshly brewed strong coffee	Chocolate Ganache (see Chocolate Sauce, page 144)
5 eggs (separated)	

In our catering kitchen this dessert ranks as No. 1 favourite among chefs and servers alike. Approach the recipe in stages: make the cake and mousse 1–2 days ahead, and then make the ganache and assemble on the day you wish to serve. It is excellent served with fresh raspberries or strawberries.

Method

Preheat oven to 180°C. Line a sponge roll tin with baking paper and grease paper with baking spray or melted butter.

Place chocolate and coffee in a double boiler with water in the base and simmer over a low heat until chocolate just begins to melt. Remove from heat and stir until chocolate has completely melted.

Place egg yolks in a bowl, whisking briefly, preferably using an electric mixer. Gradually add sugar, continuing to whisk until mixture is pale, fluffy and very thick. Add the warm chocolate mixture and salt to egg yolk mixture and whisk until cool.

In a clean bowl, place egg whites and whisk until stiff peaks form. Carefully fold half beaten whites into chocolate mixture and when almost combined fold in remaining half.

Pour mixture into prepared tin and gently spread. Bake for 15–17 minutes, or until cake springs back when gently touched in the centre.

Remove cake from oven and place on cooling rack. Leave in cake tin, cover with

Chocolate Mousse

Makes 775ml / Serves 6–8

125g dark chocolate, preferably 70% (buttons or coarsely chopped tablet)

60g (½ cup) cream cheese (not low fat, coarsely chopped)

70g (⅓ cup) castor sugar

1 egg yolk

300ml cream (whipped to soft peak stage)

plastic wrap and cool for 1 hour.

Invert cake leaving plastic wrap in place and remove tin.

Spread cake with Chocolate Mousse and carefully roll cake from long side, lifting plastic wrap to get it started. Place roll seam-side down and chill for at least 1 hour, overnight or, if required, freeze for up to 1 week.

Place Chocolate Roulade on serving tray and using a palette knife, or table knife, spread Chocolate Ganache onto roulade. Do not apply water or heat to the spreader as the ganache will become streaky and discoloured.

This mousse works well in Chocolate Roulade, as it has a firm set. It also works well as little desserts set in pretty glasses, or even as a frozen dessert.

Method

Place chocolate in a double boiler with water in the base and simmer over a low heat until chocolate just begins to melt. Remove chocolate from heat and stir until chocolate is completely melted. Cool.

Place cream cheese, sugar and egg yolk in the bowl of a food processor fitted with a metal blade and process until mixture is smooth and sugar is dissolved.

Pour chocolate through feed tube of food processor and process until mixture is combined.

Quickly transfer chocolate mixture to a large bowl and gently fold in cream. Chill for at least 1–2 hours, but preferably overnight.

Coffee and Chocolate Choux Pastries with Chocolate Sauce

Makes 12

110g unsalted butter (diced)

250ml (1 cup) water

140g (1 cup) flour (sifted)

4–5 eggs (lightly beaten)

600ml Coffee Pastry Cream and Chocolate Pastry Cream

Chocolate Sauce (see page 144)

fresh raspberries (optional)

Coffee Pastry Cream and Chocolate Pastry Cream – Makes 600ml

1 vanilla bean (cut lengthways in half)

500ml (2 cups) milk

250g (1¼ cups) sugar

60g (⅓ cup + 2 tbsp) flour

6 egg yolks

30ml (2 tbsp) very strong freshly brewed coffee

60g dark chocolate, buttons or coarsely chopped tablet, preferably 70%, partially melted

185ml (¾ cup) cream (lightly whipped)

Sometimes there is an occasion that calls for a big, rich dessert. This is the dessert for those occasions with the added bonus that components can be pre-prepared and then assembled just when your guests are ready to eat. The Coffee Pastry Cream and Chocolate Pastry Cream can also become fillings for prebaked pastry cases, served in small glasses with berries or layered between thin sheets of sponge.

Method

Preheat oven to 200°C.

Line a baking tray with baking paper.

Place butter and water in a saucepan over a medium heat and bring to the boil.

Remove saucepan from heat and add flour all at once. Mix with a wooden spoon and stir continuously until mixture separates from sides of saucepan.

Allow to cool for 5 minutes.

Place mixture in bowl, preferably of an electric mixer fitted with a paddle beater, and gradually add eggs, beating well between each addition. You may not need 5 eggs – aim for a paste with a dropping consistency (when scooped up with a spoon, it should fall off in blobs rather than run freely). Beat for 5 minutes or until paste is smooth and shiny.

Place paste in a piping bag fitted with a 1cm plain nozzle and pipe pastries onto prepared baking tray, making each 5cm in diameter and 4 concentric circles of paste high. Alternatively, use 4 level tablespoons of paste, one on top of the other, to form 5cm rounds.

Place in oven and bake for 25–30 minutes or until pastries are light golden brown.

Remove pastries from oven and prick with a metal skewer on 2 sides.

Reduce oven temperature to 180°C. Place pastries back in oven and bake for 15–20 minutes until they are golden brown, crisp and dried out.

Place onto wire racks to cool. Store in an airtight container for up to 3 days, freeze, or proceed to next step.

Cut choux pastries horizontally through the centre, leaving two-thirds as the base and one-third as the top. Place bases on platter or individual plates.

Fill some bases with Coffee Pastry Cream and some with Chocolate Pastry Cream. Place tops back on.

Generously drizzle each pastry with warm Chocolate Sauce and serve. Accompany with fresh raspberries if you wish.

To Make Coffee Pastry Cream and Chocolate Pastry Cream
Place vanilla bean and milk in a heavy-based saucepan over a medium heat and bring to the boil.

In a separate bowl, place sugar, flour and egg yolks and whisk until pale. Slowly pour milk with vanilla bean into egg mixture, whisking continuously as you pour.

Wash saucepan. Transfer mixture to the saucepan. Stir over a low heat until mixture comes to the boil, reduce heat and simmer for 2 minutes until thick and creamy.

Pour mixture through a sieve into a clean bowl using back of a soup ladle. Rinse vanilla bean and reserve for further use.

Divide pastry cream into 2 portions.

Fold coffee into half of pastry cream, and chocolate into other half, and cool to room temperature.

Cover with plastic wrap to sit directly on top of mixture, rather than covering bowl, and place in refrigerator until completely cold. This will keep for several days in refrigerator but does not freeze well.

Just before serving, divide whipped cream in half and fold one portion into the coffee pastry cream and the other portion into the chocolate pastry cream.

Photograph on following page: Coffee and Chocolate Choux Pastries with Chocolate Sauce

Marmalade Baklava with Orange Syrup

Makes 1 x 24cm round pastry / Serves 10–12

50g Michael's Brown Bread Praline (see page 143)

110g (13 tbsp) pistachios (toasted and roughly chopped)

100g (¾ cup) dried cranberries

32 filo pastry sheets (you will need around 1½ packets)

100g butter (melted)

170g (½ cup) marmalade (Cumquat Marmalade on page 142 makes this delicacy very special)

300ml Orange Syrup

Orange Syrup – Makes 300ml

110g (½ cup + 2 tsp) sugar

150ml (½ cup + 1 tbsp + 2 tsp) water

60g (3 tbsp) Tawari or a light floral-flavoured honey

65ml (4 tbsp + 1 tsp) orange juice

zest of 3 oranges

A small piece of this baklava as dessert after dinner, or in the afternoon with tea or coffee, is very satisfying as it is sweet and fruity without the richness associated with many desserts. Store covered at room temperature for up to three days.

Method

In a small bowl, combine Michael's Brown Bread Praline, pistachios and cranberries.

Place filo pastry sheets on a flat surface and, using the base of a 24cm cake tin as a guide, with a sharp knife cut filo pastry into rounds (32 rounds are required).

Cover pastry rounds with a damp cloth to prevent drying as you work. Wrap and refrigerate or freeze leftover pastry for another use.

On a flat surface place one pastry round and brush lightly with butter. Repeat the process until there are 10 pastry rounds in a stack. Lift pastry stack and place into the base of a 24cm springform cake tin.

Spread pastry stack with 2 tablespoons of marmalade.

Sprinkle evenly with one-quarter of the praline mixture.

Place 2 rounds of filo pastry on a flat surface and brush with melted butter. Cover with a further 2 rounds. Place these 4 rounds on top of the praline. Repeat this process of layering pastry, marmalade and praline until you have 4 praline layers.

Place the remaining 10 filo pastry rounds on top of the final praline layer buttering every other sheet, including the top.

Cover well with plastic wrap and chill in refrigerator 30 minutes or overnight.

Preheat oven to 180°C.

Remove baklava from refrigerator and with it still in the tin uncooked cut into 10–12 even-sized wedges. Brush top layer again with melted butter.

Place in oven and bake for 30–40 minutes or until golden in colour.

Remove baklava from oven and pour Orange Syrup evenly over the top (some syrup will run into cuts but do not deliberately pour into cuts).

Allow baklava to stand and absorb syrup for at least 2 hours before serving.

Store covered at room temperature.

Orange Syrup
In a small saucepan over a medium heat, place sugar, water, honey, orange juice and orange zest. Stir until sugar has dissolved.

Bring to the boil, turn the heat down and simmer very gently for 5 minutes until syrupy.

Remove from heat and let cool.

Blackbottom Pie

Makes 1 x 23cm pie / Serves 8–10

375ml (1½ cups) milk

125ml (½ cup) cream

4 egg yolks

12g (4 tsp) cornflour

100g (½ cup) sugar

30ml (2 tbsp) dark rum

5ml (1 tsp) vanilla essence

85g dark (70%) chocolate (buttons or coarsely chopped tablet)

1 x 23cm Sweet Short Pastry Case, baked blind (see page 119)

6g (2 tsp) gelatine powder

45ml (3 tbsp) cold water

2 egg whites

10g (1 tbsp) sugar

Chocolate Shards for garnish (optional)

Chocolate Shards

150g dark chocolate (buttons or coarsely chopped tablet)

This pie was continuously on the menu at Marbles Restaurant in Kelburn, the restaurant I owned for 10 years in the late 70s and 80s. It is still a much-admired pie with its pastry base filled with a layer of deeply rich chocolate custard topped with lighter rum and vanilla custard. There are always occasions that call for a pie such as this.

Method

Pour milk and cream into a medium-sized, heavy-based saucepan and bring to the boil over a medium heat.

While milk and cream are heating, place egg yolks and cornflour in a bowl and whisk together for 1–2 minutes, or until just combined. Add sugar and continue whisking until mixture is pale yellow and holds the mark of the whisk.

Slowly pour milk and cream into egg mixture, whisking constantly. Add the rum and vanilla and return mixture to the saucepan.

Over a medium heat, bring custard almost to the boil, stirring with a wooden spoon. Reduce heat to low and simmer, stirring for 5 minutes or until custard thickens. Pour custard into a bowl so that it does not continue to cook.

Place 375ml (1½ cups) of custard into a smaller bowl and add chocolate. Stir until chocolate is melted.

When chocolate custard is cool, pour into pastry case. Refrigerate while making the rest of the filling.

Place gelatine and cold water in the bowl for approximately 5 minutes or until the gelatine has softened. The gelatine will absorb the water. Gently heat softened gelatine until it dissolves and becomes clear. I do this in a microwave on medium for 25 seconds.

Mix dissolved gelatine into remaining custard and chill until almost set …

... Blackbottom Pie

... Whisk egg whites and slowly pour in the second measure of sugar. Continue whisking until soft peaks are formed. Gently fold egg whites into the vanilla custard and spread evenly over chocolate custard in the shell.

Refrigerate for at least 2 hours or until firm. If you wish, garnish with chocolate shards.

To Make Chocolate Shards
Place chocolate in a double-boiler with water in the base and simmer over a low heat until chocolate is just beginning to melt.

Remove from heat and stir chocolate until it is all melted.

Line a flat oven tray with aluminium foil. Pour chocolate onto tray and, using a dry metal spatula, spread the chocolate out to a rectangle about 25 x 20cm and 3mm thick. Sit chocolate in refrigerator for 10–15 minutes until set and brittle.

Remove chocolate from refrigerator. Pick up slab of chocolate and with dry, cold hands, break roughly into shards. If not using immediately, store in an airtight container with baking paper between layers.

Sweet Short Pastry Case

Makes 1 x 23cm case

200g (1⅓ cup + 1 tbsp) flour + extra for dusting bench	3 tbsp castor sugar
½ tsp salt	50ml (3 tbsp + 1 tsp) cold water (approx.)
100g (1 tbsp) unsalted butter (diced)	baking spray or olive oil for greasing flan tin
1 egg yolk	

The pastry for this case can be made several days in advance and stored in the refrigerator for two weeks ahead or frozen. I like to make several discs of pastry at one time and freeze the excess until required.

Method

Sift flour and salt into a large bowl and add butter to flour.

Lightly rub butter into flour until it resembles fine breadcrumbs. Make a well in the centre.

In a measuring jug, whisk together the egg yolk, castor sugar and cold water until the sugar is dissolved. Pour a little of the egg mixture into the well and gradually incorporate the flour and butter, adding more egg mixture as necessary, to make a smooth, firm paste.

Knead pastry into a disc shape, wrap in plastic wrap and rest for at least 30 minutes, or overnight, in refrigerator before rolling.

Grease a removable-bottomed 23cm flan tin with baking spray or oil. On a lightly floured bench, roll pastry to a 30cm circle, 2mm thick. Carefully place pastry into flan tin by rolling it loosely over the rolling pin, picking it up, and rolling it over flan tin. Press pastry into shape without stretching it, being careful to exclude any air (allow the edges of pastry to overhang flan tin).

Rest pastry for a further 20 minutes. Preheat oven to 150°C.

To bake pastry case blind, cover pastry with aluminium foil and then fill the cavity with dried beans or rice. Bake pastry case for 10–15 minutes or until pastry is pale but set.

Remove the aluminium foil and dried beans or rice and trim over hang of pastry from the flan case. Return flan tin to oven and bake case for a further 10–20 minutes or until the pastry is golden brown and cooked through.

six

Baking

There is an urban myth that no one likes to bake any more. However, that doesn't quite stack up because I receive more responses about baking than any other kind of recipe. There is a big crowd of people out there who adore baking – and eating it. To be worth the time and the calories, baking needs to be really tasty. In the following section you will find treats literally bursting with flavour.

Apricot and Almond Tarts

Makes 12 tarts

		For the filling
flour for dusting bench and trays	1 egg (separated)	250g (1 cup) cream cheese (diced)
650g puff pastry (buy the most buttery version you can find)	1 tbsp water	1 egg yolk
	25g (¼ cup + 1 tbsp) sliced almonds	50g (4 tbsp) brown sugar
6–9 Poached Apricots (see page 124)	40g (4 tbsp) sugar	40g (¼ cup + 2 tbsp) ground almonds (lightly toasted)
	whipped cream (optional)	

These tarts also work well with other fresh fruit such as pears, plums or peaches. They can be frozen, unglazed and unbaked, and glazed and baked from frozen. Allow 2–3 minutes extra cooking time from frozen but don't increase temperature.

Method

Dust bench with flour and roll pastry to a 2–3mm thickness.

Using a straight-edged pastry cutter or a saucer, cut 12 x 9.5cm rounds for the tart bases and 12 x 12cm rounds for the tart tops.

Lay out the pastry bases on greased trays and pastry tops onto lightly floured trays.

Place a tablespoonful of filling into the centre of each pastry base, dividing filling evenly among the 12 bases but leaving an uncovered rim around the edge of each.

Place half to three-quarters of an apricot, depending on size of apricots, on top of filling.

Lightly beat the egg white and brush uncovered rim of each pastry base. Place top on each tart and crimp edges together. Completely seal using fork prongs.

Place tarts in refrigerator to rest for 20–30 minutes.

Preheat oven to 200°C.

Lightly beat egg yolk with 1 tbsp water. Brush tops of tarts with egg yolk.

Sprinkle generously with sliced almonds and sugar.

Bake for 12–15 minutes or until golden brown and crisp.

Serve with whipped cream, if you wish.

To make filling

Place cream cheese in a bowl and beat until smooth. Add egg, brown sugar and almonds and beat until combined.

Poached Apricots

400–600g (6–9) apricots

300g (1½ cups) sugar

750ml (3 cups) water

Apricots will bob above the surface of the syrup as they cook. Cut a round piece of greaseproof paper the diameter of the saucepan and place directly on top of the syrup to keep apricots immersed. Poached apricots are an exquisite dessert served with Vanilla Bean Ice Cream (see page 103) and Raspberry Sauce (see page 145).

Method

Cut apricots in half lengthways, following the natural line of the apricot. Remove stone and discard.

In a wide saucepan, place sugar and water over a medium heat. Stir until sugar is dissolved. Increase heat and without further stirring bring syrup to the boil.

Add apricots to syrup, cut side up. Bring syrup back to the boil, reduce to a medium heat and simmer apricots on one side for 2–3 minutes or until they are tender but not soft. Cooking time will depend on the ripeness of the apricots.

Remove apricots from syrup. Retain apricot syrup for further fruit poaching.

Serve warm, or set aside to cool to place in Apricot Almond Tarts.

Fresh Date and Cream Cheese Friands

Makes 12

baking spray or melted butter for greasing moulds	155ml (½ cup + 3 tbsp) egg whites
250g (12) fresh dates	2 tsp finely grated lemon zest
40g (4 tbsp) cream cheese	
225g (1½ cups) icing sugar (sifted)	155ml (½ cup + 3 tbsp) clarified butter (warm but not hot)
70g (½ cup) flour (sifted)	
1 tsp ground cinnamon	icing sugar to serve
130g (1¼ cups + 1 tbsp) ground almonds	

Friands are best eaten on the day they are made but are still perfectly acceptable a couple of days after baking. In our catering kitchen we often freeze friands in their moulds unbaked and then bake them from frozen as required. Allow 2–3 minutes additional baking time but don't increase the temperature.

Method

Grease friand moulds with baking spray or melted butter.

Cut down one side of each date to remove stone and create a cavity for cream cheese.

Transfer cream cheese to small piping bag (without nozzle) and pipe to fill date cavity or alternatively, using a table knife, scrape cream cheese into cavity, rounding the top. Close dates.

Preheat oven to 180°C.

Into a large bowl sift together icing sugar, flour and cinnamon.

Add ground almonds, egg whites (not whisked) and lemon zest and stir to combine.

Slowly pour in clarified butter, gently folding until butter is entirely incorporated.

Spoon half the mixture evenly into prepared moulds. Place one filled date lengthwise into centre of each mould and cover with remaining friand batter.

Bake for 20–25 minutes until light golden brown and slightly pulling away from the sides of the moulds. They should still be a little moist. Only when they are overcooked do they bounce back when prodded …

... Fresh Date and Cream Cheese Friands

... When cool enough to handle, remove from moulds. Sift extra icing sugar over friands and serve.

To Clarify Butter

Place butter in a small saucepan and melt butter slowly over a low heat.

Remove from heat and slowly pour butter through a fine sieve, leaving white milk solids in base of saucepan. Discard milk solids.

The sieve will capture any scum off the top of the butter that has formed during the clarification process. Set aside to cool for 5–10 minutes before using, or store in refrigerator.

Spanish Toast with Sherry Raisins

Serves 3–6	**Sherry Raisins**
125ml (½ cup) good-quality Spanish dry sherry	200g (1⅓ cups) raisins (washed)
2 eggs	water for covering raisins
4 tsp castor sugar	150g (¾ cup) sugar
4 tsp cinnamon	60ml (4 tbsp) water
olive oil	90ml (6 tbsp) good-quality Spanish sweet fruity sherry
½–1 brioche loaf (cut into 6 x 1.5cm thick slices)	1 tsp lemon zest
Sherry Raisins	

Enjoy this for an absolutely decadent celebration brunch that takes very little work. To get organised make the raisins ahead and have a brioche loaf in the freezer. Make extra raisins to keep in refrigerator to serve with chocolate or vanilla ice cream.

Method
Pour sherry into a small bowl.

Break eggs into another small bowl and whisk until fluffy.

Combine castor sugar and cinnamon in another small bowl.

Pour enough oil into a shallow, heavy-based frying pan to form a depth of at least 1cm and heat to medium-hot.

Dip brioche into sherry then immediately into egg mixture.

Immediately place into frying pan and fry for 1 minute on each side, or until golden brown. Remove from oil and transfer onto paper towels to drain.

Dip warm Spanish Toast into sugar and cinnamon mixture and serve warm with Sherry Raisins.

To Make Sherry Raisins
Place raisins in a small saucepan and cover with cold water.

Over a medium heat, bring to the boil and cook for 5 minutes or until raisins are plump and juicy.

Strain and rinse under cold water. Discard liquid.

In a clean saucepan combine sugar and water and, over a low heat, stir until dissolved. Bring to the boil and cook for 2–3 minutes, or until a syrupy consistency is reached.

Remove from heat and cool. Add sherry, lemon zest and raisins and stir to combine.

Store in an airtight container in the refrigerator.

Passionfruit Honey, Lime and Blueberry Cake

Makes 1 x 25cm cake

baking spray or melted butter for greasing tin	210g (1½ cups) flour
170g unsalted butter (diced and softened)	1½ tsp baking powder
	½ tsp salt
300g (1½ cups) sugar	250ml (1 cup) Passionfruit Honey (see page 141)
4 eggs	40g (6 tbsp) ground almonds
15ml (1 tbsp) lime juice	
3 tbsp finely grated lime zest	300g blueberries (fresh or frozen)
30g (½ cup) thread coconut (toasted)	Vanilla Yoghurt Cream (optional) (see page 143)

New York caterer and cookbook author Serena Bass baked her son Sam's wedding cake, a lemon curd cake, in our kitchen. We loved Serena's cake but recipes often metamorphose. We adapted Serena's recipe to come up with this cake.

Method

Preheat oven to 180°C.

Line a 25cm round cake tin with 2 layers of baking paper and grease paper with baking spray or melted butter.

Place butter and sugar into a bowl. Beat until light and fluffy. (I like to use an electric mixer.)

Add eggs, one at a time, beating between each addition.

Add lime juice, lime zest and coconut and beat to combine.

In a separate bowl, sift flour, baking powder and salt. Fold into egg mixture with a spatula.

Pour into prepared cake tin and smooth out the edges.

Spread Passionfruit Honey over cake batter, leaving a 1cm rim around the outside of the cake.

Sprinkle ground almonds evenly over Passionfruit Honey and top entire cake with blueberries.

Bake for 55–65 minutes, or until cake, when gently shaken, does not wobble in the centre.

Serve warm or cold with Vanilla Yoghurt Cream. Best eaten on the day it is made but it is delicious for up to 2 days.

1.

2.

3.

Diet-be-damned Brownie

Makes 40 squares

baking spray or melted butter for greasing tin	5 eggs (lightly beaten)
105g (¾ cup) flour	5ml (1 tsp) pure vanilla extract or essence
60g (½ cup + 2 tbsp) cocoa (preferably Dutched cocoa)	555g (3⅓ cups + 2 tbsp) dark chocolate, preferably 70% (buttons or coarsely chopped tablet)
340g (1 cup + 9 tbsp) unsalted butter (cubed)	
590g (2¾ cups + 1 tbsp + 1 tsp) castor sugar	icing sugar for dusting

Be warned, this is addictive. Save any trimmings or broken pieces to use in Diet-be-damned Brownie Ice Cream (see page 105). Dutched cocoa, cocoa powder ground from cocoa beans which have been treated with an alkali solution, is milder, less acidic and darker than untreated cocoa.

Method

Preheat oven to 180°C. Line the base of a 33 x 23cm sponge roll tin with teflon sheet or baking paper. Grease the sides of the tin with baking spray or melted butter.

Sift flour and cocoa into a medium-sized bowl.

Place butter in a saucepan over a low heat. Add sugar and stir until sugar is dissolved. Cool slightly. Add eggs and vanilla and stir until combined.

Add flour mixture and chocolate. Mix well.

Pour mixture into prepared sponge roll tin and bake for 40–45 minutes, or until crusty on top and firm to touch. A skewer inserted will come out slightly sticky.

Gently run a knife around the edges to loosen brownie from tin.

Allow brownie to cool completely in tin before turning out onto a cooling rack and remove teflon sheet or baking paper.

Place on a firm, flat board and with a large knife trim edges and cut brownie into 4cm squares.

Place brownies in an airtight container with greaseproof paper between each layer. Store at room temperature for up to 1 week, or in freezer for up to 3 months.

Allow brownie to come to room temperature if it has been frozen, and when you are ready to indulge, dust with icing sugar.

Pumpkin Cupcakes with Cream Cheese Frosting

Makes 24–30 little cupcakes

baking spray or melted butter for greasing tins

2 eggs

100g (1 cup) sugar

125ml (½ cup) salad oil

245g (1 cup) steamed and mashed pumpkin (chilled) (325–375g raw, peeled pumpkin is needed to make 1 cup cooked pumpkin)

140g (1 cup) flour

1 tsp baking powder

¼ tsp salt

½ tsp ground cloves

1 tsp ground cinnamon

¼ tsp ground ginger

pinch freshly ground nutmeg

5 walnuts (toasted and chopped)

5 dried apricots (finely chopped)

5 tsp pumpkin seeds (roughly chopped)

370g Cream Cheese Frosting

Cream Cheese Frosting – Makes 370g

25g (1 tbsp + 2 tsp) butter (softened)

125g (½ cup) cream cheese (cubed)

225g (1½ cups) icing sugar

¾ tsp pure vanilla extract or essence

1½ tsp lemon juice

These little cupcakes are moist and tasty and just the right size to enjoy with a tea or coffee. Freeze unbaked in tins if required and bake from frozen, increasing baking time by 3–4 minutes.

Method

Preheat oven to 180°C. Grease baby muffin tins with baking spray or melted butter.

Place eggs and sugar in a bowl and whisk until mixture is combined. Add oil and pumpkin and combine.

Sift in flour, baking powder, salt and spices and stir until just combined but making sure all the lumps are dissolved.

Pour mixture into prepared muffin trays to three-quarter-fill tins. Bake for 15 minutes until a skewer when inserted comes out clean.

Leave in tins for at least 5 minutes before turning onto a cake rack to cool.

In a small bowl, combine walnuts, apricots and pumpkin seeds and set aside.

Once cold, ice cupcakes on their bases with Cream Cheese Frosting and sprinkle with walnut mixture.

To Make Cream Cheese Frosting

Place butter and cream cheese in a bowl and beat until well combined.

Sift in icing sugar, add vanilla extract and lemon juice and continue beating until icing is smooth.

Chocolate Toasted Sandwiches

Makes 8 sandwiches

50g (5 tbsp) unsalted
butter (softened)

8 slices fruit bread

1 tsp cinnamon

80g (½ cup) dark
chocolate, preferably
70% (buttons or coarsely
chopped tablet)

icing sugar for dusting

Serve for brunch, morning tea or for a quick dessert. These moreish little treats are loved by both adults and children.

Method

Generously butter one side of each slice of bread.

Cover work surface with plastic wrap. Place bread, buttered side down, onto work surface.

Evenly sift cinnamon over the bread.

Cover 4 slices of bread with chocolate and top with second slice of bread, buttered side up. At this stage you can place sandwiches in refrigerator in a container lined and layered with plastic wrap until you are ready to cook.

Heat a heavy-based frying pan, grill plate or panini machine to medium-hot. Place sandwiches in frying pan and cook for 2–3 minutes until golden brown. Turn sandwich over and cook for a further 2–3 minutes.

Remove from frying pan onto a baking tray and keep warm under a clean tea towel as you continue to cook.

Using a serrated-edged knife, cut each sandwich in half.

Sift icing sugar over sandwiches and serve warm.

Golden Queen Scones with Passionfruit Glaze

Makes 24 small scones

baking spray or melted butter for greasing trays

350g (2½ cups) high-grade flour

85g (⅓ cup + 2 tbsp) sugar

½ tsp salt

1 tbsp baking powder

175g (½ cup + 5 tbsp) cold butter (diced)

185ml (¾ cup) milk

235g (1⅔ cups) chopped Golden Queen peaches

Passionfruit Glaze

100g (½ cup) sugar

125ml (½ cup) passionfruit pulp (obtained by scooping out passionfruit or purchasing frozen pulp)

Golden Queen peaches are a very flavoursome variety and keep their shape when cooked. When peaches are out of season make these scones using fresh pineapple.

Method

Preheat oven to 190°C. Grease 2 flat or low-sided baking trays with baking spray or melted butter.

Into a bowl, sift flour, sugar, salt and baking powder.

Add butter and combine until mixture resembles coarse breadcrumbs. (You could do this by hand or using the paddle attachment of an electric mixer.)

Add milk and peaches and mix gently until just combined. Do not over-mix as the dough will become tough.

Using an ice cream scoop or soup spoon, scoop batter onto prepared trays.

Place trays in oven and bake for 15–20 minutes until tops are firm but not hard and scones are golden brown in colour. Scones will spring back when gently pressed in the centre.

Remove scones from oven and drizzle with warm Passionfruit Glaze.

If possible serve warm.

To Make Passionfruit Glaze:

Place sugar and passionfruit pulp in a small saucepan set over a low heat and stir until sugar is dissolved. Bring to the boil, then remove from heat.

seven

Sauces & Condiments

It's the little bits and pieces, the extras, which make dishes really special. Sauces & Condiments contains my favourite embellishments for dressing up food, guaranteed to impress your guests.

Cranberry Chutney

Passionfruit Honey

Makes 875ml

500g frozen cranberries (defrosted)

160g (1) apple (peeled, cored and diced)

400g (2 cups) brown sugar

185ml (¾ cup) white vinegar

90g (½ cup) mixed peel

½ tsp salt

¼ tsp ground ginger

¼ tsp ground cloves

¼ tsp ground allspice

¼ tsp dry mustard powder

Makes 435ml

3 eggs

200g (1 cup) sugar

50g (5 tbsp) butter (cut into cubes)

125ml (½ cup) passionfruit juice (obtained by straining passionfruit pulp)

This is a great chutney to serve with turkey or ham, or to give to friends at Christmas-time but it can be enjoyed all year round, particularly as an accompaniment to brie.

Method

In a large, non-reactive saucepan, place cranberries, apple, brown sugar, vinegar, peel, salt, ginger, cloves, allspice and mustard.

Place over a low heat and stir until sugar is dissolved.

Bring to the boil then reduce heat to a simmer. Cook for a further 20–25 minutes, stirring from time to time, until chutney has reduced, is syrupy and fruit has begun to break down.

Pour into sterilised, hot jars and seal.

Store in pantry.

This is useful to have on hand to fill little pastry cases, drizzle over pavlova, or to combine with cream cheese to make a frosting.

Method

Place eggs and sugar in a microwave-proof jug and whisk until combined.

Add butter and passionfruit juice and whisk briefly. Cook on high for 6–8 minutes, whisking after every minute, until mixture is smooth and creamy.

Cool for a few minutes then pour into a clean container. Once cold, cover and store in refrigerator for up to 1 month.

Cumquat Marmalade

Makes about 1l

1kg cumquats (washed)

750ml water

sugar

A cumquat tree in the garden or in a pot is a very decorative plant but has the added bonus of producing citrus fruit which make the most flavoursome of all marmalades. Thank you to Stephanie Alexander in *The Cook's Companion* for getting me started on Cumquat Marmalade.

Method

Discard cumquat stems and thinly slice cumquats, flicking out and reserving pips as you go.

Tie pips in a small piece of muslin.

Place fruit, pips and water in a large ceramic or stainless steel bowl. Leave overnight to soak.

For every cup of fruit and soaking water, use 1 cup of sugar, e.g. if you have 3 cups of fruit with soaking liquid you will need 3 cups (600g) sugar.

Pour fruit with soaking liquid and pips tied in muslin into a large, non-reactive

preserving pan and place over a medium heat for 10–20 minutes, stirring from time to time until fruit is tender.

Add sugar and stir over medium heat until dissolved.

Increase heat and boil for about 25 minutes until marmalade reaches setting point. To determine if setting point is reached, place a few drops of marmalade onto a chilled saucer and place the saucer in the freezer for 2 minutes. If the drops have retained their shape on the saucer, it has reached setting point.

Remove marmalade from heat and let sit for 10–15 minutes. Stir to encourage even fruit distribution.

Remove pips tied in muslin and discard. Pour marmalade into hot sterilised jars and seal while still hot. Store in pantry.

Michael's Brown Bread Praline

Vanilla Yoghurt Cream

Makes 100g

50g (1–2 slices) stale wholemeal bread

30g (3 tbsp) unsalted butter

50g (¼ cup) sugar

½ tsp cinnamon or allspice

Makes 560ml

250ml (1 cup) cream

125ml (½ cup) yoghurt

1½ tsp vanilla extract or essence

Michael Lee Richards often serves this sweet, crispy, crunchy topping on chocolate mousse. Thanks to Michael we store his praline in the freezer as a standby and serve it on many fruit dishes.

Method

Crumble bread but not too finely. In a small frying pan over a medium heat, melt butter and add bread. Cook until crisp, stirring occasionally.

Sprinkle bread with sugar and spice. Continue to cook, stirring frequently until crumbs begin to caramelise and are a pale golden colour.

Transfer praline to a low-sided tray and leave to cool. Store in an airtight container for up to 2 weeks.

Combining yoghurt with cream provides an acidic but rich foil for many cakes. Serve this cream very chilled.

Method

Pour cream into a small bowl and whisk until soft peaks form.

Add yoghurt and vanilla and fold into cream. Serve immediately.

Chocolate Sauce

Makes 350ml

200ml (¾ cup + 2 tsp) cream

200g (1¼ cups) dark chocolate, preferably 70% (buttons or coarsely chopped tablet)

Serve hot or warm and make sure you have plenty.

Method

Place cream in a small saucepan and bring to just below boiling point.

Remove from heat, add chocolate and stir until chocolate is melted and sauce is silky smooth.

To Make Chocolate Ganache

To acheive the perfect silken finish to many cakes, leave Chocolate Sauce at room temperature for around 30 minutes, or until mixture sets to a spreading consistency.

Caramel Sauce

Makes 385ml

300g (1½ cups) brown sugar

150g (½ cup + 2 tbsp + 1 tsp) unsalted butter (diced)

235ml (¾ cup + 3 tbsp) cream

1 tsp vanilla extract or essence

Serve this sauce with Sticky Banana Puddings (see page 98) or use in ice cream sundaes with banana or pineapple, or drizzle over carrot, pumpkin or apple cakes.

Method

In a small saucepan, place sugar, butter, cream and vanilla and mix together.

Place saucepan over a medium heat and stir until butter is melted and sugar is dissolved.

Simmer for 4–6 minutes or until sauce has slightly thickened.

Use immediately, or when cool, store covered in refrigerator. Gently reheat but do not allow to come to the boil.

Raspberry Sauce

Tawari Honey and Pinot Noir Lavender Sauce

Makes 350ml

300g fresh raspberries, or thawed from frozen

100g castor sugar

juice of ½–1 lemon

15ml (1 tbsp) Crème de Framboise (raspberry liqueur) or Crème de Cassis (blackcurrant liqueur) (optional)

Serves 8 / Makes 375ml

870ml (3½ cups) pinot noir

250ml (1 cup) Tawari honey or another light floral honey

4 tbsp (¼ cup) finely chopped shallots

4 tsp finely chopped fresh lavender leaves or 1 tsp dried culinary lavender flowers

flaky sea salt and freshly ground black pepper

A very handy sauce to serve over ice cream, fruit salad or with anything chocolate. Crème de Framboise, raspberry liqueur, really heightens the flavour of the raspberries.

Method

Place raspberries and sugar in the bowl of a food processor fitted with a metal blade and process until pulped.

Strain through a sieve to remove seeds, pushing on pulp with back of soup ladle.

Add lemon juice to taste and Crème de Framboise or Crème de Cassis, if you wish.

We designed this sauce to go with Duck Breast (see page 68) but find it equally delicious with lamb. Only use English varieties of lavender, such as *Lavandula angustifolia* or *Lavandula intermedia* for cooking. French varieties are more showy in the garden but too soapy in flavour and aroma for cooking.

Method

In a small saucepan, combine pinot noir, honey, shallots and lavender and place over a medium heat. Bring to the boil and reduce heat. Simmer until sauce has reduced by two-thirds.

Season with salt and pepper, strain and serve immediately or reheat to serve.

Fresh Tomato Sauce

Makes 600ml

2kg (10–15) ripe tomatoes (roughly chopped)	2 cloves garlic (finely chopped)
water	½ dried red chilli (deseeded)
1 tbsp flaky sea salt	
30ml (2 tbsp) extra virgin olive oil	1 sprig rosemary and sage (tied together)
20g (2 tbsp) butter	½ tsp freshly ground black pepper
20g (2) shallots (finely chopped)	12 basil leaves (sliced)

This tomato sauce recipe, suitable for pasta or pizza, was given to me by an Italian friend, Peter Daldin, who lives nearby in Otaki. Peter is a fine cook and gardener. He likes to use a mix of tomatoes from his garden in this sauce – acid-free, beefsteak or rounds. Use in Roasted Eggplant, Red Pepper and Zucchini Lasagne with Puy Lentils (see page 43), spread onto uncooked pizza bases, or toss through pasta.

Method

Place tomatoes into a large saucepan and cover with water. Bring to the boil, reduce heat and simmer for 5–10 minutes.

Drain, then return tomatoes to saucepan with 1 cup of water and 2 tsp salt. Cover and bring to the boil. Strain again and discard water.

Push tomatoes through a mouli to make purée.

In a medium-sized saucepan, place oil and butter and melt butter. Add shallots, garlic and chilli. Cook for 2–3 minutes or until shallots and garlic are soft but not brown.

Add tomato purée, rosemary and sage, 1 tsp salt and pepper to the shallots.

Place a lid partially on saucepan and bring to the boil. Remove lid, turn heat down and simmer for 1 hour or until thick enough to coat pasta, stirring occasionally to ensure sauce does not stick to base of saucepan. Remove herb sprigs and add basil. Season to taste.

Old-fashioned Tomato Sauce

Makes about 2.5l

2kg ripe tomatoes

500g apples (golden delicious, gala or other sweet apples)

500g onions (peeled)

4 tbsp whole cloves

2 tbsp whole allspice

1½ tbsp whole black peppercorns

500g (2½ cups) sugar

2 tbsp flaky sea salt

¼ tsp cayenne pepper

1¼ cups malt vinegar

This is my version of a classic recipe in *Digby Law's Pickle and Chutney Cookbook* published by Hachette Livre.

Method

Coarsely chop tomatoes, apples and onions. Tie cloves, allspice and peppercorns in a small piece of muslin.

Place all ingredients into a preserving pan or large, heavy-bottomed, non-reactive saucepan.

Bring to the boil and cook uncovered for 1 hour or until sauce is mushy and slightly thickened.

Put sauce through a mouli, or pass through a sieve using a soup ladle to press down on solids.

Wash pan and pour sauce back into pan and slowly bring to the boil. If you would like a thicker sauce, reduce heat and simmer until sauce reaches required consistency. Remove from heat and pour into sterilised and still-hot jars or bottles. Seal and store in pantry.

Semi-dried Tomato and Lemon Dressing

Makes 310g

125ml (½ cup) olive oil

15ml (1 tbsp) balsamic vinegar

finely grated zest of 1 lemon

30ml (2 tbsp) lemon juice

1 clove garlic (crushed)

150g (¾ cup) semi-dried tomatoes

4 tbsp chopped Italian parsley

flaky sea salt and freshly ground black pepper

This dressing will keep refrigerated in a covered container for one week. In addition to serving with Baked Ricotta Cake (see page 14), you can also serve dolloped onto bruschetta or grilled steak or fish.

Method

Into a small bowl place olive oil, balsamic vinegar, zest and lemon juice, garlic, tomatoes and parsley.

Combine with a fork and season to taste.

Roasted Garlic

Orange, Cumin and Mint Vinaigrette

4 heads of garlic

olive oil

3 sprigs of thyme

flaky sea salt and freshly ground black pepper

Makes 130ml

1 clove garlic (chopped)

½ tsp flaky sea salt

½ tsp cumin seeds (lightly toasted)

½ tsp coriander seeds (lightly toasted)

15ml (1 tbsp) orange juice

1 tsp finely grated orange zest

15ml (1 tbsp) sherry vinegar

¼ tsp paprika

½ red chilli (halved, deseeded and finely chopped)

90ml (6 tbsp) olive oil

1 tbsp roughly chopped mint leaves

1 tbsp roughly chopped coriander leaves

Roasted Garlic is used in Garlic Mashed Potatoes with Thyme Crumbs (see page 85) but it is also a useful ingredient to have on hand to add to sauces, dressings and dips or to use as a spread on bruschetta.

Method

Preheat oven to 180°C. Trim top quarter off whole garlic heads to expose cloves. To remove bitterness, place in a small saucepan of boiling water set over a medium heat to cook for 10 minutes. Drain. Discard any loose skin and puncture sides and top with a fork.

Place in a small ceramic dish and drizzle generously with oil then sprinkle with thyme, salt and pepper.

Place in oven and roast for about 40 minutes or until cloves start popping out of skins.

When garlic has cooled or when you are ready to use it, squeeze out pulp from skin.

This is a flavoursome vinaigrette for Vegetable Salad (see page 91). It is a gutsy dressing so is also perfect served drizzled over lamb or chicken dishes.

Method

In a mortar place garlic, salt, cumin seeds and coriander seeds and crush to a dry paste with a pestle. Alternatively, make a paste in a small food processor. Transfer to a small bowl.

Add orange juice, orange zest, sherry vinegar, paprika and chilli and whisk together.

Add oil and whisk to combine. Add mint and coriander and stir to combine. Season to taste.

Cover and chill for at least 1 hour for flavours to infuse. Store covered in refrigerator.

Red Wine and Balsamic Sauce

Apple Shallot Sauce

Makes 360ml

250g (1¼ cups) brown sugar

250ml (1 cup) red wine

45ml (3 tbsp) balsamic vinegar

280g (20) shallots (peeled and halved)

4 cloves garlic (smashed)

Makes 500ml

350g (2) Braeburn apples (peeled, cored and cut into 12 wedges)

145g (16) small shallots (peeled)

40g (8) garlic cloves (peeled and halved)

750ml (1 bottle) sauvignon blanc

250ml (1 cup) tart apple syrup (there are several brands available in the supermaket)

5ml (1 tsp) balsamic vinegar

12–24g (1–2 tbsp) brown sugar

When I serve this sauce with Beef Wellington (see page 65) I strain the caramelised shallot and garlic out and retain for separate use. With the shallots and garlic in the sauce it is perfect to serve with grilled steaks.

Method

Into a small stainless steel saucepan set over a low heat place brown sugar, red wine and balsamic vinegar. Stir until sugar is dissolved.

Add shallots and garlic and continue to cook over low heat for 10–15 minutes until shallots are soft and liquid is reduced by about half.

Serve immediately or reheat to serve.

Serving this sauce with Rosemary and Fennel Seed Roast Leg of Pork (see page 62) cuts down on the stress of making last-minute gravy. The clean, fresh flavours of the sauce break through the richness of pork. It is gravy and apple sauce all in one. Serve with other pork dishes such as pork sausages or pork belly.

Method

Into a medium-sized, non-reactive saucepan place apples, shallots, garlic, wine and apple syrup.

Bring saucepan to boil over a medium heat. Reduce heat and gently simmer for 40–45 minutes or until liquid is syrupy and apples, shallots and garlic are soft.

Add balsamic vinegar, then remove from heat and add brown sugar to taste.

Serve immediately or reheat to serve.

Sandwich Mayonnaise

Avocado and Herb Dip

Makes 625ml

4 egg yolks

1 clove garlic (peeled and halved)

flaky sea salt and freshly ground black pepper

2 tsp wholegrain mustard

juice of 1½ lemons

60ml (¼ cup) salad oil

440ml (1¾ cups) salad oil

Makes 250ml

1 ripe avocado (cut in half and stone removed)

1 clove garlic (crushed)

2 tbsp finely chopped parsley

1 tbsp finely snipped chives

2–4 drops Tabasco sauce

30ml (2 tbsp) lemon juice

45ml (3 tbsp) sour cream

15ml (1 tbsp) extra virgin olive oil

flaky sea salt and freshly ground black pepper

This is the mayonnaise we always have on hand in our catering kitchen for cocktail sandwiches.

Method

Place egg yolks, garlic, salt and pepper to taste, mustard, lemon juice and first measure of oil into bowl of a food processor with metal blade fitted. Process until smooth.

Place remaining oil into a jug and very slowly pour oil through feed tube of processor while machine is running.

Season to taste. Store tightly covered in refrigerator for up to 5 days.

Serve with Parmesan Chicken Skewers (see page 13), or use as a dip with vegetable sticks, or toasted Pita Crisps (see page 21), or as an accompaniment to grilled fish or chicken.

Method

Peel avocado and roughly chop.

Into the bowl of a food processor fitted with a metal blade place avocado, garlic, parsley, chives, Tabasco sauce, lemon juice, sour cream and oil. Process until creamy but not necessarily smooth and add seasoning to taste.

Place dip in a serving bowl and serve, or cover with plastic wrap onto surface of dip and chill for 1–2 hours before serving.

Garlic Béchamel Sauce

Makes 580ml

500ml (2 cups) milk

3 cloves garlic

35g (3 tbsp + 1 tsp) butter (diced)

30g (4 tbsp + 1 tsp) flour

100ml (⅓ cup + 1 tbsp) cream

flaky sea salt and freshly ground black pepper

This silky smooth sauce is the binding sauce in Roasted Eggplant, Red Pepper and Zucchini Lasagne with Puy Lentils (see page 43). Add chopped parsley or tarragon to this sauce and serve it with poached chicken. Add grated gruyère and serve with steamed cauliflower.

Method

Pour milk into a heavy-based saucepan and add garlic. Place over a medium heat and bring to the boil.

Remove from heat and cover. Leave for 15 minutes so garlic infuses milk.

Place butter in a second saucepan and melt over a medium heat. Add flour and stir to combine. Cook for 2–3 minutes or until it smells nutty. Strain milk through a sieve. Discard garlic and pour milk into mixture.

Simmer sauce over a very low heat for 20 minutes, stirring occasionally. (Place a SimmerMat under the saucepan if you have one.)

Pour in cream and season to taste.

Refrigerate in covered container. To prevent skin forming, place plastic wrap directly on top of sauce.

Basil Pesto

Lemon-infused Olive Oil

Makes 120ml

1 clove garlic (peeled)

50g (⅓ cup) pine nuts

45g (½ cup) basil leaves

45g (⅓ cup) finely grated Parmesan

50ml (¼ cup) olive oil

flaky sea salt and freshly ground pepper

lemon juice to taste

Makes 250ml

250ml (1 cup) light olive oil (this is available in supermarkets. 'Light' refers to the flavour)

¼ cup finely grated lemon zest

Make when basil is plentiful so you have lots of pesto on hand in the freezer during winter.

Method

Into the bowl of a food processor fitted with a metal blade, place garlic, pine nuts, basil and Parmesan. Process until smooth.

Through the feed tube, with processor going, slowly pour in olive oil.

Add salt, pepper and lemon juice to taste.

Store in an airtight container in refrigerator for up to 2 weeks, or freeze until required.

This is such a useful condiment. Try it on beans, asparagus, broccoli or zucchini. Brush it onto fish or seafood before cooking or season and use as a salad dressing.

Method

Place oil and lemon zest in a bowl. Stir, cover and place in refrigerator for up to 4 days so that the zest can infuse the oil.

Strain oil through muslin, discard zest and store oil in a sterilised jar in refrigerator for up to 4 weeks.

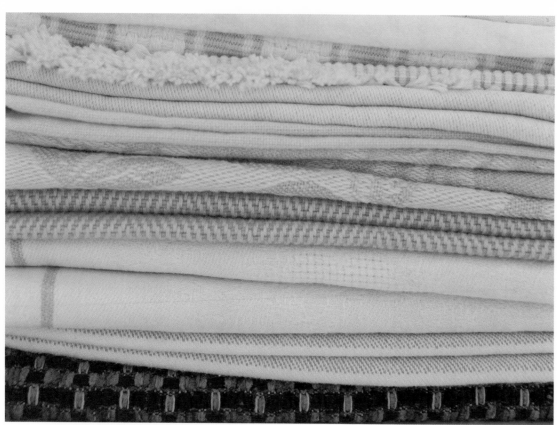

For contributing dishes and
utensils used in this book,
thank you to:

Kirkcaldie & Stains Ltd
165–177 Lambton Quay
Wellington

Andrew Hawley Ltd
36 Tacy St
Evans Bay
Wellington

La Maison
142 Featherston St
Wellington

nest wellington
16 Woodward St
Wellington

For menu suggestions, please
visit: www.ruthpretty.co.nz

Index